Hungry for Love

Psychological Tidbits to Nourish an Empty Heart

E. Edward Reitman, PhD

BookPartners
Wilsonville, Oregon

To Harriet
For forty-three years my most severe critic
and my constant support.

Nourishment for the tummy,
Nurturance for the soul,
Thoughts to think over,
Prepared to help you get whole.

E. Edward Reitman

Table of Contents

Acknowledgments

I am fortunate to be able to view my world as a wonderful buffet, highlighted by a loving wife, devoted children with their spouses, and three beautiful and unique grandchildren. That alone would be sufficient to fulfill my emotional plate. However, I am additionally blessed by a large array of loving friends, who have always been there to provide help, advice or a quiet, reassuring presence. There is also a small circle of very special individuals who have served as major emotional pillars of support in my life. You know who you are.

Three other people were especially influential in the writing of this book. First, of course, is Harriet, who has always had more faith in me than I have ever had. For that, I can never thank her enough.

Second, Katherine Blissard, who as hostess of *This Day With Katherine* on Houston television dubbed me the "This Day Psychologist" and had me on her show at least once or twice a week for more than eight years. She not only introduced me to the media but she, along with Ann Hodges, *Houston Chronicle* TV critic, opened my eyes to the notion that I could write. Third, Tony Vallone, master chef, proprietor of six of Houston's best restaurants, including Tony's—one of the finest eating establishments in the country—but most of all, one of my dearest friends. Over the years he has generously shared with me his knowledge and passion for food and its preparation. He is always there to gently instruct and support my culinary attempts, even when they fall short of the mark.

I also want to thank Mollie Ehmling for her patience during the times she typed the many drafts of this manuscript over and over and over again. Additionally, my appreciation goes out to Thorn and Ursula Bacon and their staff at BookPartners, Inc., for their publishing know-how and to Dave Lindstedt whose editorial skills helped to shape the manuscript into its final form.

Lastly, more than I can possibly express in words, my thanks go out to my patients, who lived through the ordeal of my writing this book and supplied many of the examples. They also encouraged and pushed me to complete it. Time and time again they threw my own words back to me: "Run toward the things you fear." My heartfelt thanks goes out to each and every one of you.

Introduction

Most of us can recall our mother, grandmother or close relative who shared her love by putting food on our plates. The tidbits she prepared were more than food for the stomach, they were emotions for the soul and love from their hearts. In a similar fashion, *Hungry For Love* is a psychological platter of provocative thoughts to nourish your soul and recipes to whet your appetite. Each chapter deals with everyday issues that we encounter in the course of trying to find love in our relationships with our friends, family, children, or spouse.

Using food analogies to foster communication and understanding, I have tried to weave together insights from therapy, sound psychological concepts, personal experiences, and common sense to provide positive guidelines for living and loving. My hope is to help you live life better, communicate more effectively, and develop a greater insight into yourself. My intent is to present sometimes difficult concepts in a palatable manner and to leave you with some thoughts to arouse your mind and emotions and give you a sense of hope for your future.

This isn't a book that you must read in one sitting. The bite-size chapters allow you to nibble on a morsel when you have a few moments to spare. If you find something meaningful to think about, or some insight into yourself or your relationships, then I will have achieved my objective. To keep the tone light and to reinforce my theme that building loving relationships is similar to cooking a delicious meal, I have included a special recipe at the end of each chapter. Although not every dish is heart healthy, each recipe is emotionally healthy. I have personally prepared every recipe for guests whose reactions were enthusiastically positive. Moreover, they are all easy to prepare and you can rest assured that they will serve to enhance your confidence in your culinary ability and heighten your reputation as a host or hostess.

More importantly, *Hungry For Love* reminds you that it is never too late to grow, to change or to make your life more enjoyable. Whatever the nature of your problems or your circumstances in life, I believe that every one of us can learn new attitudes and behaviors. This book shows you how to start.

Chapter 1

Junk Food, Junk Health, Junk Emotions

❊ ❊ ❊ ❊ ❊ ❊ ❊ ❊ ❊ ❊ ❊ ❊ ❊

Have you ever stopped to marvel at the magnificence of your body? Just for a moment, consider the complexity of its parts and the many services it provides. Underneath your skin, which itself is a sophisticated climate-control system, lies a cogeneration plant, changing one form of energy into another; a mainframe computer not yet invented by man; a chemical refinery; a recycling facility; and a two-way electrical network. Each of these facilities has been designed to operate both individually and collectively to control and integrate the physical, intellectual, and emotional processes of life. I've given you a mouthful of words but they only begin to describe the wonder of the human body. It took some masterful engineering to create our bodies and enable them to adapt and function in an ever changing environment.

We are not self-perpetuating pieces of machinery, however. Without proper fuel in the form of food, water, and air, our bodies cease to operate. Moreover, the quality of the fuel affects the level of performance. The cleaner, the purer, the less contaminated the air we breathe, the water we drink or the food we eat, the more efficiently and effectively our bodies function. The proper mixture of quality fuel and exercise contributes to a healthier body, a clearer mind, a happier disposition, and a longer life.

When you look in the mirror, you may not see the finely tuned, expertly crafted body described above. Unfortunately, many of us have allowed our bodies to fall into disrepair through poor diet, lack of exercise and other forms of neglect. Acceptance of a lower quality of fuel has become so widespread in the United States that we've created a term to describe it: junk food. The fatter, the sweeter, the better. In the name of convenience and expedience, the result of this trend is that many of us are putting junk food into our bodies and reaping junk health in return.

My purpose is not to launch into a tirade about junk food. Heaven knows that most of the recipes I've included wouldn't qualify as low-fat, low-calorie health foods. My point is to remind you that you have the ability to choose what you consume in life—and your decisions will make all the difference in the quality of your life and your relationships.

In much the same way that your body depends upon diet and exercise to function well, your "heart"—the symbolic seat of emotions and feelings—needs to be fed and exercised, or it ceases to work properly. If you feed it love, compassion and joy, and exercise it by caring for others and nurturing relationships, your heart can be tuned to function in a sensitive, responsive and caring manner. It can exude warmth and concern, and can help you and others to feel a sense of security and safety in a sometimes frightening world.

On the other hand, if you feed your heart junk food, such as petty grievances, fear of the unknown, spite, anger, greed, selfishness, envy, insecurity and depression, it will still function (our hearts are very adaptable), but it will leave behind a trail of noxious fumes consisting of pain, guilt, hostility and grief that can emotionally poison everyone in close proximity.

There is no doubt that if we put junk emotions in, only junk feelings will result. But life need not be a series of problems covered by a shroud of sorrow and misery. I know from so many of the patients I have seen over the years, when they initially looked at their world all they could see was darkness and upset. Later, when they learned that they were in control of what they chose to consume, both physically and emotionally, step by step they began to feed themselves better. They recognized hope in the world. They admitted that they wanted to be loved and they realized that they had to risk asking for love. In other words, they learned that love is available to all of us, but we have to harvest it before we can take advantage of it.

No matter what you have been fed until now, you have the ability to choose what you will feed your heart from now on. We all can learn to fuel our hearts with quality love for ourselves, to have high hopes and to experience and express positive emotions toward the people in our lives and the activities we choose. These are the positive emotional foods that we need to consume.

Spicy Sausage Bread

This might be called junk food, but it makes a wonderful appetizer to serve with drinks. It is much like Italian calzone and makes a nice lunch accompanied by a salad or a bowl of soup. The amount of red pepper flakes can be adjusted to taste. Makes two loaves.

1 lb. hot Italian sausage, casings removed (in a pinch I
    have substituted Jimmy Dean's Hot Sausage and
    couldn't tell the difference)
2 cups shredded mozzarella cheese
2 cups grated cheddar cheese
3/4 cup minced onions
1/3 cup minced green bell peppers
1/3 cup minced red pepper
1/3 cup finely chopped celery
1 teaspoon crushed red pepper flakes
2 16-oz. loaves frozen bread dough, thawed
3 tablespoons melted butter

Preheat oven to 350°. Cook sausage in a large heavy skillet over medium high heat until almost brown, about 4 minutes. Drain all but two tablespoons of oil. Add onions, peppers, celery, and pepper flakes and continue cooking for 2 to 3 minutes. Allow pan to cool, then add cheese, and mix well. While pan is cooling, roll each loaf of dough out on a flour-coated surface to a 9" x 16" rectangle. Spread half of sausage mixture evenly over each piece of dough, leaving a 2" border. Starting at the long side, roll up like a jelly roll. Remove each roll to a greased baking sheet, brush with melted butter and bake approximately 40 minutes until golden brown. Cut slices and serve warm.

Chapter 2

Peeling the Onion

❋ ❋ ❋ ❋ ❋ ❋ ❋ ❋ ❋ ❋ ❋ ❋ ❋ ❋

Once a couple came to me for therapy after only six weeks of marriage. They were already talking about divorce. In the month-and-a-half since the wedding, they had fought and argued more than they ever had during the entire year they had been dating and engaged. Before they were married they had lived in different cities and had only seen each other on weekends, holidays, and whenever possible in between. Now that they were together under one roof, life had turned into a constant battle.

They came to therapy as the result of "an argument over nothing." Beverly said that Mike had flown off the handle when she came home late from work one night. From Mike's perspective it was simply one more example of how inconsiderate, lacking in understanding and impossible to deal with she was. "You're a poor wife and completely insensitive to my needs," he had told her.

Enraged by his attack, she had pulled off her wedding ring and had thrown it at him. She was fed up with his belittling, critical remarks, his fault-finding attitude, and his attempts to control and demean her. "It's been nothing but pain since we got married," she had said, "and I can't take it anymore."

Later, after the argument had ended and Mike had gone upstairs, Beverly went back to the living room to look for her ring. She couldn't find it. After several minutes of searching, she decided she would look the next morning when she was less upset. She didn't panic, because she knew the ring had to be there somewhere.

When the couple awoke the next morning, the atmosphere was still as cold as the Arctic. Beverly was leaving on a two-day business trip that morning, and after working around each other getting dressed and exchanging a few curt, monosyllabic statements, Mike left for work and Beverly caught a cab to the airport. Before she left, she forgot to search for the ring. She promised herself she would look when she got home, but it seemed as soon as she walked in the door, she and Mike were embroiled in another terrible fight.

He was irate that she had paperwork to complete after being gone for two days. He accused her of being far more involved with her job than with him and said that if that was the way she wanted it...

She protested tearfully, almost overwhelmed by the fear that she was losing him. When she vocalized her concern, he suddenly produced the ring and screamed "Is that right? Three days ago you lost your wedding ring and you never even searched for it. You never asked me to look for it—nothing! You don't care about a thing. Nothing matters to you except yourself, your job and your own selfish needs."

Such was the happy atmosphere surrounding their first counseling session. Both Beverly and Mike were hurt and defensive. Neither one understood what was really going on. They told their stories angrily and couldn't seem to see any deeper than their own outer skins. If there was to be any solution, they desperately needed to peel away the tough, protective covering that guarded their tender inner selves but also made them unpalatable and unattractive to others.

Much like peeling the outer skin of an onion to get to the edible meat of the bulb, in order to see ourselves the way we truly are as humans, and to show our true selves to those who are close to us, we must peel away the defensive layers that we show to the world. Mike and Beverly needed to recognize what they were feeling and acknowledge how they were acting. Then they needed to find ways that were far more clear and less confrontational to express who they were, what they were, and what they needed.

Peeling the outer skin involves time and considerable effort, and much like peeling an onion, the process will bring tears to your eyes. It took Mike and Beverly a long time to learn how to look inside themselves rather than point the finger at one another. And it will require even more time for them to see themselves honestly enough to share their true selves.

For starters, I led them through a role-playing exercise, where I spoke for them. I modeled a manner of speaking that I hoped they would be able to speak on their own within a year. I spoke in a way that demonstrated letting their guard down. Every one of us is capable of hiding behind a thick outer shell. Some of us are worse than onions. Some are artichokes, with thorny outer leaves; or coconuts with very hard shells.

In playing the role of Mike, I said "Beverly, I'm sorry I yelled and screamed and put you down. I don't want to lose you. I love you. I care for you. I know my behavior doesn't demonstrate or reflect it. But I'm so hurt. You see, I'm not just the big business executive that everybody sees on the outside. The man you married is a guy who never felt loved as a kid, a guy who puts on a tough, outer shell to hide his desperate feelings of loneliness and emotional neediness. I want you to love me. I want you to care for me. I want to feel that I come first for you. I know you can't make me feel that way, but you could contribute by helping me get to a place where I can feel that way.

"I need to know I'm important to you. I need to know that if you lose your wedding ring, even if you throw it at me in a rage, you care enough to look for it. Maybe I deserved to have the ring thrown back in my face, but I want you—ten minutes, an hour, two hours later—to do your best to find it. You even could have asked me to help look for it; but instead, I picked it up the next day. Then I put it away and waited for you to panic over losing it. I waited for you to say, "Mike, what am I going to do? I lost my ring and it's important to me to find it." But three days later it still wasn't important. You never came to me, you never even mentioned it. I felt like the ring was more important to me than it was to you.

"So I decided to turn the tables on you When I left for work today, I deliberately left my ring right by the sink where you could see it. What did you do? You came running out yelling, 'Put this on. This is no way to work on a marriage.' Well I'll be damned. You're telling me to wear my ring. You're telling me to work on a marriage that you don't even care about. That's why I went into a rage. I don't want to live the way I've lived all my life, feeling unimportant and in second place. I want to be able to come home, let my sails down, let all the wind out and find a safe harbor.

I want to know that you're there for me, that it's safe and that you won't attack or hurt me. I need to know that you will love me and care for me and nurture me. All I can tell you is that I hurt desperately. I saw your lack of concern for the ring and I assumed it meant a lack of concern for me and our marriage. I need for you to assure me that that isn't the case."

Then I spoke to Mike on Beverly's behalf, saying what I believed she was feeling: "Mike, I don't want to hurt you. I don't want our relationship to end. I don't want a third bad marriage. I ran from my other two relationships and rightfully so. One man ran around on me and the other was an alcoholic.

"I feel like such a failure. All my life everybody has looked at me and said, 'Beverly, you're strong, you're capable, you're tough. You don't need anybody. You can handle life on your own. You were always good at sports. At school. At people. At work.' Sure I was good; I was trying hard to be good in order to be loved. Still, it never seemed to matter; all the love and attention went to my siblings, who were in trouble more times that I can begin to count. I guess the squeaky wheel really does get the grease.

"Then I got into a marriage and I was scared from day one. I know I married losers the first two times, maybe even on purpose. But you're not a loser; I love you and I want you. But I'm so scared. And if lack of love or appreciation hurts *you,* I feel destroyed when you yell and scream and holler at me. You see, I'm really not that strong. I'm not able to take care of myself in emotional relationships. I'm a runner, but anytime you see me start to run, I'm begging you to stop me. Give me a kiss. Tell me you care. It doesn't take much. Just once in my life I want to be able to believe that I come first in somebody's eyes. I'm as hungry for love as you are. I just hope we can understand each other's hurt and give each other the love that we both want."

The ability to speak from the heart and to demonstrate outwardly our inner emotions is the best example I can give of peeling away our protective outer skins. It is analogous to cutting off the tough outer leaves of an artichoke or cracking the shell of a coconut. It is the path to the meaty part of an onion, the soft, delicate heart of an artichoke, and the meat and milk of a coconut.

Even though I strongly advocate the peeling of our outer skins, I want to emphasize that the facades, or skins, that we took so long to develop are not without value and shouldn't be totally discarded. To the contrary, our outer skins do have worth. In the world of food, we can pickle the rind of a watermelon, or use the thin layer of skin from a lemon or lime to add zest to many dishes. If we boil the peelings from potatoes, onions, and turnips, we make vegetable broth that can be used as the base for wonderful gravies and soups.

If we apply some warmth to our peelings—to cook them, in a sense—we may soften their outer texture and bring out hidden flavors. The defense mechanisms that we developed early in life truly serve a purpose. Rightly applied in adulthood, they can continue to be of value. For example, when a person who has hidden throughout his life behind a veil of humor peels away the facade, he can still use his sense of humor to help him communicate more effectively. Likewise, the person whose best defense was once a very strong offense can use the "gravy" of an outgoing, forceful personality to enhance a career in sales. By "cooking" our tough exteriors through a process of self-discovery and learning how to show the goodness and softness that lives within us, we create a delicious "broth" that adds flavor to our lives and to the lives of those around us.

If we desire to have close, meaningful, loving relationships, we have no choice but to open ourselves up to the heat that naturally goes along with intimacy. Once again, think in terms of an onion. A raw peeled onion leaves a sharp, biting flavor on your tongue, is heavy on your breath, and makes your eyes water. But the same onion exposed to the heat of a sauté pan adds a pungent, smoky flavor to foods. Granted, jumping into the frying pan entails the risk that you might get burned, and it might be one of the most difficult steps you ever take, but—trust me on this—it is the surest path to finding out that you are loved and appreciated for who you truly are.

Red Onion Pizza

In the kitchen, as in life, once the onion has been peeled, the possibilities are endless for creating delicious and enjoyable recipes (or relationships).

This red onion pizza is something I threw together when some friends dropped by the house one evening. I had the shell and some red onions on hand, and everything blended together very well. It's fast, easy and somewhat unique. It'll bring tears of joy to your eyes as you watch your friends enjoy it.

1 large packaged pizza shell
1/4 cup + 1 tablespoon virgin olive oil
4-5 cloves garlic (minced)
2 medium red onions (thinly sliced)
3 tablespoons sliced black olives
1/4 teaspoon red pepper flakes, or to taste
1/3 cup Parmesan cheese

Preheat oven to 400°. Spread one tablespoon of olive oil on shell with pastry brush. Place on center rack in oven approximately 4 minutes until shell is slightly browned. Meanwhile sauté onions in remaining olive oil with red pepper flakes and garlic until the onions are soft but not browned. Remove from heat and mix in black olive slices. Spread mixture evenly over pizza shell. Sprinkle with Parmesan cheese and return to oven for approximately 5 to 6 minutes. Remove from oven and cut into 3" x 3" squares to make it easier to serve as an appetizer.

Chapter 3

Faith and Watermelon Seeds

About thirty-two years ago, when my son David was four-and-a-half or five, I had the itch to get my hands into the soil when spring arrived. One morning, I was on my way to the garden shop and, seeing an opportunity for a little bonding, I invited David to come along. I thought it would be good for the two of us to get involved in something constructive together. We went to the nursery and I picked out my starter plants—tomatoes, basil, oregano—along with seed packets for cucumbers, string beans, carrots, parsley—the kinds of things I knew for sure would grow.

When I had finished making my selections, I looked at David, spun the rack around and said, "Now, what do *you* want to plant? Would you like to plant my cucumbers?" (I knew he would experience some success with them.) "What about some zucchini?" David shook his head solemnly and began to scan the array of seed packets on the rack in front of him. Suddenly, his eyes opened wide and with a quick glance at me he reached for an envelope of watermelon seeds. I thought to myself, *I have never seen watermelons grow in a small, backyard garden.* I knew he would never have success with these seeds, but after a good deal of fruitless cajoling, convincing, rationalizing, and arguing, I bought the watermelon seeds and we loaded everything up in the car. What I should say is, I loaded everything up while David clutched his precious envelope of watermelon seeds.

By the time we got home, it was too late to finish the entire garden, so I planted the starter plants and stored the envelopes of seeds in the garage. I promised David that the next weekend we would plant his watermelon seeds. "Meanwhile," I said, "let me tell you two of the most important things you will have to do. First, you'll need to water your seeds. You see, just like people, plants get thirsty. They need to be able to drink. Also, just like people, plants need to eat. What we have to do is give them a little fertilizer, which makes them strong and helps them to grow into watermelons or cucumbers or tomatoes." I was still trying to get him to switch to a surefire grower like cucumbers, but I could tell by his eyes that the only thing on his mind was gigantic green watermelons.

As I finished my little speech, I thought, *okay, we'll try it. You never know. Even if we don't get watermelons, at least we'll get a vine, maybe a flower or two and he can feel that he accomplished something.* Later that week, I came home one night to find a large empty area in the middle of the lawn I had been cultivating for endless weekends in a row. The grass was gone. Just then, David rushed up and grabbed my hand, anxious to show me where he had planted his watermelon seeds. You guessed it. With my wife's help, he had started his watermelon patch smack dab in the middle of the lawn. I bit my lip and, as a psychologist, reminded myself that kids are more important than grass.

The following weekend, I planted the remainder of my seeds.

Several weeks later, tender green sprouts provided tangible evidence that the seeds had germinated. I showed David how to water, fertilize, and pull weeds, providing what the young plants needed for growth and removing those things in each plant's environment that might hurt or strangle them. Similarly, David and I cared for his watermelon patch. Though we repeatedly had to get rid of grass that wanted to return to the open wound in the lawn, nothing else grew—no vines, no leaves, no indication of any kind that the watermelons were going to sprout.

My first inclination—as a father, certainly not as a psychologist—was to question whether he had watered them enough. I felt the ground and it seemed appropriately moist. He hadn't drowned the seeds. "Maybe you put too much fertilizer on them," the father in me said. (I had to blame someone, didn't I?) But it didn't appear as though too much fertilizer had been added

We waited another few weeks and my plants were growing like crazy. My tomato plants had little yellow flowers on them, but there was still only a bare spot in the middle of the lawn. Occasionally I said to David, "Maybe we should plant something else, something you can watch grow."

His answer was always the same: "No, they're fine, they're okay."

"But David, I'm afraid they are not going to grow. Please think about planting something else."

One evening when I was tucking him into bed, I turned to him again and said, "David, how do you know the watermelons are okay? Maybe they just died."

He looked at me as only a child can and said, "I just know they're okay."

"Yes, but how?" I asked

"Every day, I dig them up and look at them just to make sure."

There was the answer. His care and concern had caused them to die. He had examined them, inspected them, and controlled them to the point that he took away their opportunity to grow.

We sometimes make the same mistake in the course of raising our children, developing close friendships and establishing marital relationships. Often, we undermine our relationships not because we don't care or because people don't matter, but because we care too much. In the process of trying to acquire the relationship we desire, we sabotage the very thing we want by strangling and restricting the other person. We jeopardize our relationships when we critically examine the other person and their behavior, or become too possessive, too controlling or too demanding.

I met a woman once, whom I'll call Sandy, who was a glowing example of smothering love. From the moment they were born, Sandy zealously guarded her children. She rationalized her protectiveness by saying, "Things are different today than when I was growing up. You just can't be too careful."

She compensated for what she considered her husband's lack of understanding and sensitivity by playing the role of both mother and father. When the kids played sports, she was always there to cheer them on. When they needed to be car-pooled, she trusted no one but herself to drive them. She checked their homework every night, all the while complaining that her husband didn't care. She monitored the children's phone calls and scrutinized their rooms and desk drawers. All pant pockets were turned inside out before washing, and she always made sure to check with the other parents when her kids spent the night out.

After the kids got their driver's licenses, they were given beepers so that they could be located at any time. Whenever they drove anywhere, they were required to call her upon their arrival and to let her know when they were leaving and where they were going.

On the surface, much of her behavior appeared to be very caring. To many mothers, she was the perfect parent. However, though she truly loved her children, her motivation was love for herself, not for them; and the extent to which she was involved was unquestionably excessive.

Her husband would jokingly say, "I'm in sixth place, behind the kids, the house and the dog." Despite his attempts at humor, the marriage relationship was strained at best. I believe he unconsciously resented and was jealous of his children's involvement with their mother. As a result, he became critical, hostile, and estranged from his entire family.

Eventually the kids themselves began to resent their mother's behavior, which they perceived as over-controlling. One child (the so-called good one) became mildly obese. He experienced severe interpersonal problems, was awkward and fearful in relationships with young women, and appeared clinically depressed. For him, his mother's love was truly crippling. He couldn't live with it and he was afraid to live without it.

His brother (the "bad one") failed in school and developed a drug problem. Although he had little difficulty in developing heterosexual relationships, they always included covertly hostile behavior. He was consistently late or failed to show up at all for dates. When he made plans with a young lady, he would frequently "forget," and he refused to be pinned down to any kind of schedule.

In the midst of all this turmoil, Sandy was dumfounded. She couldn't understand how she could dedicate her entire life to her home and her children and have the end result be that both of her children were having problems and her husband was threatening to leave. She concluded that it doesn't pay to love anyone. She found it nearly impossible to accept any responsibility. "After all," she said self-righteously, "what more could I have done?"

Perhaps it wasn't a case of what more she could have done, but rather what less she might have done.

When John came to see me, his feelings were similar to Sandy's. His first wife, Melissa, had left him when their last child went off to college. She said she was tired of being controlled, criticized and unappreciated. From John's perspective, *he* was the one who was unappreciated. "When I first met my wife, she was unsophisticated and unedu-cated—still wet behind the ears. In many ways, you could say I took her on to raise. After all, her parents certainly hadn't done a very good job."

Now, eight years later, Melissa is happily remarried, but history seems to be repeating itself for John. His new wife was shy, sensitive, and dependent when he met her, but she didn't stay that way very long. During her first visit to my office, I encountered a bright, sensual, extremely attrac-tive young woman, twenty years John's junior. She was completing her senior year in college and seemed confident that she would be accepted into law school the following year. Although she claimed to love her husband, she added, "I am sick to death of his looking over my shoulder, never allowing me to make my own mistakes, and checking and rechecking my checkbook and credit card charges. He is just like my mother."

John began to see the handwriting on the wall, but unfortunately he reacted to his fears rather than changing his actions. He intensified old behaviors already guaranteed to fail. Rather than look at himself, he chose to scrutinize his wife for faults or problems. If anything, he tightened his control over her daily schedule, based on his suspicion that she might be involved with someone else. Sadly, this type of behavior often results in pushing their partner into the feared behavior. Then the only consolation is to be able to say, "See, I knew what was going on all along," which is a terrible price to pay in order to be right.

In many ways, both John and Sandy acted like my young son with his watermelon seeds. Instead of trusting that their spouse or their children would grow and bear good fruit with proper nourishment and care, they smothered, stifled, controlled and examined their "seeds" until they ended up with a bare patch in the lawn of their relationships—and no watermelons.

If you see yourself in this example, it's time to make some emotional and behavioral adjustments. Years ago a patient said to me, "You are so lucky. All your patients love you for being there during their time of need, for supporting them and for guiding them. It must be a wonderful feeling." It is a wonderful feeling. But the love I really cherish is when a patient leaves therapy and no longer needs me, but still values me. Like a bird sitting on your shoulder, love is far more meaningful when the bird is free to fly away rather than tied to you.

If you give up the illusion of control and allow others the room to grow—to make their own decisions and their own mistakes—you'll find that your offspring and your spouse love you more for who you are than for what you do. Have faith in your ability to sow good things, nurture your relationships with the confidence that one day the things you've sown will grow and produce good fruit that you can enjoy.

Each of us has something of worth to give that is both meaningful and nurturing to others. Although we won't necessarily reap the fruit immediately, over time the harvest of good relationships is certain to come in.

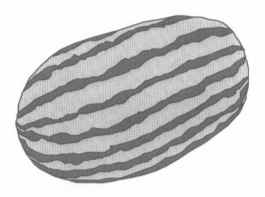

Watermelon Gazpacho

If you can't grow a watermelon in your own backyard, grab a juicy one from your local market. Watermelon is one of my favorite summer treats. Just slice it, sprinkle on a little salt, and I'm in heaven.

That's not much of a recipe, so I searched until I found several for watermelon sorbet. I tested a few, but the results lacked taste, substance or distinct identity. As my father-in-law would say, "I wouldn't leave home for it."

I also considered a recipe for pickled watermelon rind, but the end product wasn't worth the amount of work involved.

Finally I came across a watermelon recipe that might not inspire you to leave home but will definitely serve as a wonderful appetizer for a hot summer night's meal. And your guests will be amazed when they finally guess the main ingredient.

10 cups 1-inch watermelon cubes, red part only, without
    seeds. Discard drained juice
3 slices toasted white bread crumbs
1 each: green, red, and yellow bell pepper, seeded and
    minced
1 medium onion, minced
1 jalapeño pepper, seeded and minced (optional)
4 garlic cloves, minced
2 medium cucumbers, peeled, seeded and minced
2 cups chopped Italian flat parsley
1/4 cup red wine vinegar
1 tablespoon virgin olive oil
1 or 2 pinches cayenne pepper to taste
salt and freshly ground black pepper to taste

Cut melon in cubes and puree in food processor or blender. Pour into large bowl. Add toasted bread crumbs, minced peppers, onion, jalapeño, garlic, cucumber, parsley, vinegar and oil and stir. Add salt, pepper, and cayenne to taste. Chill before serving. It is best to serve the same day it is made. Serves 12.

Note: requires approximately an 8 pound seedless watermelon.

Chapter 4

Truth in a Pot of Gumbo

It might have been the best gumbo I ever made. It should have been. I stood for what seemed like hours stirring the roux until it was silky, thick, and a beautiful dark brown. I couldn't have been more pleased with my efforts. No microwave shortcuts or bottled roux would do for me. They couldn't begin to compare to the contents of my cast iron skillet. I had taken particular care to mince the onions, green pepper, garlic, celery, and okra as evenly as possible. Just looking at the array of ingredients was a joy to behold. The aroma that permeated the kitchen would have pleased the finest Cajun cook. As the broth simmered, and I folded in the roux and added the sautéed vegetables, several cans of plum tomatoes, and various spices, I knew why cooking was such a joy.

I must admit that when I initially tasted the gumbo, I detected a slightly peculiar aftertaste, but I dismissed my concerns as readily as they had occurred. You know how sometimes something can taste bad at first when in fact it's only your taste buds acting up. Besides, Harriet—my wife and best critic—hadn't noticed a problem, and I promise you she would have been the first to let me know if anything was truly wrong.

Despite a nagging feeling in the back of my head, I added the pièce de résistance: five pounds of large shrimp, peeled and deveined, and a half gallon of shucked oysters.

I was jazzed and ready for a gumbo to end all gumbos. Nothing could be more perfect. I planned to serve half of it to our guests that evening and freeze the rest for a dinner party the following weekend. So much for best-laid plans. The longer the gumbo simmered, the stronger the aftertaste became. Upon second tasting, Harriet confirmed my worst suspicions.

I reviewed the preparation process, looking for the culprit. In the course of my investigation, I smelled the oil I had used to make the roux. Instead of the vegetable oil I had intended to use, I had grabbed a very old container of what had become slightly spoiled peanut oil. Obviously the gumbo could not be served that evening, but—still in denial—I decided to freeze it, hoping that it would lose the rancid aftertaste by the following week. Over my wife's protest, I filled every storage container in the house and packed them into every available space in the freezer.

It took me four days before I was able to forgive myself for my gross negligence. Believe it or not, this was progress. A few years ago, it would have taken considerably longer before I let myself off the hook. Nevertheless, during those four days, I beat myself up emotionally for my carelessness, my stupidity, my inability to throw things away no matter how old they are. *Five pounds of shrimp—beautiful, large shrimp—and a half gallon of oysters! How could I grab the wrong oil? And why was I keeping that rotten old stuff anyway?* Until I had sufficiently castigated myself, I was unable to accept my error as a simple mistake. Nor was I able to rid myself of the fifteen quarts of symbolic failure now jamming my freezer. Hanging on to the gumbo reminded me of my error and stifled my desire to cook, thereby preventing further failure.

Although a pot of spoiled gumbo is a relatively minor matter, the same underlying factors show up in the story of a patient of mine who had just gotten a divorce from her physically abusive husband, whom she had supported throughout most of their nine-year marriage and two-year separation. For two months after the divorce was finalized, she complained about his frequent phone calls and requests that they try again. Her grumbling lacked credibility, however, because most of her personal belongings, as well as her share of the furniture, were still stored at his house. With one foot still in the marriage, she could continue to lament the eleven years she had wasted in the relationship, cling to her resentments, and plan "sometime in the future" to get her things. Like bad gumbo in the freezer, her refusal to move on kept her grounded in the past and occupied so much space in her present that there was no room for a future.

Let's face it. Despite our best intentions and efforts, we all make mistakes. Mistakes are part of being human. We aren't perfect. The secret for living well is not to judge our adequacy as humans based on whether or not we fail or how effective we are at avoiding, denying or covering up our failures. If life is ever to be exciting, challenging, instructive, or rewarding, it will, by definition, include the risk of defeat and the occasional experience of failure. The trick to mastering life is not to avoid risk and failure, but to learn how to deal with them in a healthy, constructive manner.

Believe me, I've made bigger mistakes than using rancid peanut oil. I've twice nearly gone bankrupt, made other poor financial decisions several times, and once suffered a catastrophic loss through fire—without insurance. But what I've learned by living through adversity is that we can gain strength, we can learn how to face our fears, and we can survive our failures with hope intact and look forward to future successes.

Sometimes, using the f-word—*failure*—is a source of great relief. Take the case of Bill, an extremely handsome, intellectually gifted young man with a wonderfully pleasing personality. He had never failed to live up to his parents' highest expectations. In his mother's words, "He was the golden-haired child. If he wanted an A, he got it. When he wanted to be the quarterback, he did it. In college, he decided ahead of time which fraternity to pledge and three years later he was the chapter president. It was no different in law school, and his success continued in the firm he and several friends established after graduation."

There was one problem, however. Despite all of his accomplishments, Billy (as his parents still called him) was an extremely unhappy individual. He frequently drank to excess and lived a highly manic lifestyle.

When I first met him, he said, "It doesn't matter what I have done. Nothing gives me any real or prolonged sense of accomplishment. I hate the business of law. What I really want to do is write, but everyone tells me it's a harebrained idea."

I suggested that he test his interest by taking some creative writing courses at the university and if he found that he enjoyed writing, he might then gradually work his way out of his law practice.

The next time I saw him, he had heeded my words to excess. He had almost completely divested himself of his legal practice and was in his second semester of creative writing. He said that the professor, a man noted for his ability to develop new talent, felt he had great promise. Of course. Why would he not succeed?

Several months later, I received an emergency call from his wife, whom I had never met. She explained that during the months since I had seen him he had become increasingly depressed and was drinking more heavily. He had stopped writing and had gambled away a sizeable portion of their savings in the stock market. He had also missed two court dates for clients, whose cases were still pending. He refused to discuss any of these problems with her or with his parents.

I arranged to see him immediately. When we met, it quickly became apparent that all of these events were not happening by accident. Instead, the culmination of years of running had drained Bill's emotional gas tank. He seemed delighted by my observation that he was failing and even more pleased by my suggestion that we have a meeting with his wife and his parents. At that subsequent meeting, I suggested that he had a hidden agenda, that despite his ability to succeed in any facet of life he chose, he was actively self-destructing and failing emotionally, professionally and financially. His wife and his parents, particularly his mother, found it extremely difficult to accept my words. They were particularly incensed when I used the word "failure" in reference to Bill. He, on the other hand, seemed almost relieved. Being described as a failure gave him time to stop his endless search for success and catch his emotional breath.

Jimmy Swaggart, Jim Bakker, Gary Hart, and Bill Clinton are other examples of individuals who had it all but for whom "all" was not enough. Each, in his own way, is an exceptional person—intellectually gifted, financially and professionally successful, and nationally prominent. Each one was in a position to positively affect the lives of others, yet each eventually behaved in a self-destructive manner. With the world apparently in the palm of their hands, they let it slip through their fingers. Why? They never learned that they could fail. They never understood that they could be loved and accepted even if they weren't successful all of the time. Like many of us, they were raised on the myth that if they got the education, the success, the prominence, the money and the power, they would be happy. Each came face to face with the same disappointment and disillusionment.

They all performed well but ended up feeling bad. Although not necessarily at a conscious level of awareness, they all came to realize that outward vestiges of success are not always positively correlated with an inner sense of well being and self worth.

Nobody's perfect. What we all need to learn at a deep emotional level is that we don't have to be. As individuals, parents and spouses, we must come to the realization that we cannot live life with a fear of not succeeding, of falling short, of being human. It is the same in writing, cooking and life. First drafts are never perfect. That's why we have editors. In cooking, if you are not willing to risk a bad dish, you will never make a good one. If we bake cheesecakes, inevitably some will crack. Some of our soufflés will fall— guaranteed. And we might add a bad ingredient to an otherwise perfect batch of gumbo. But holding on to fifteen quarts of defeat and failure, and punishing ourselves for our mishaps only serves to keep us mired in the past and inhibits our growth into the future. Our failures only define us to the extent that we hang on to them. Wouldn't you rather empty the freezer and get back in the kitchen?

To live life successfully, we must learn to acknowledge our failings and then let them go. We must find ways to accept our mistakes and turn our disappointments into victories. Michael Jordan said it well: "I've missed more than 4,000 shots. I've lost more than 300 games. I have been trusted to take the game-winning shot—and missed 26 times. I've failed over and over again in my life, and that is why I succeed."

Seafood Gumbo

This is a surefire, no failure recipe—unless you have an old container of peanut oil lurking in your pantry. Chopping and mincing the vegetables requires a little extra preparation time; otherwise, it's straightforward and well worth the effort.

Roux
1-1/2 cup oil
1-1/2 cup flour
2 cups chopped onions
1 cup chopped celery
1 cup chopped bell pepper
1 cup chopped green onion
1/4 cup chopped Italian flat parsley
4 cloves minced garlic
2 lbs. frozen sliced okra

Combine the oil and flour in a heavy skillet over medium heat and stir frequently, taking care not to allow the roux to burn. Caution becomes especially important as the roux begins to reach a nut-brown color. If you are using an electric stove, turn the heat down as the roux darkens, because the element will remain hot and could ruin the roux. Adding the vegetables to the roux will also lower the heat and avoid the possibility of burning. Mix in the remaining ingredients and stir constantly until they are tender. You can freeze the roux at this point or use it immediately in gumbo.

Gumbo

1 two-pound can Italian plum tomatoes, chopped (save
        liquid)
Salt to taste
2 lbs. raw peeled shrimp
1 lb. crab meat (optional)
2 dozen small oysters (save liquid)
1 tablespoon Worcestershire sauce
1 teaspoon cayenne pepper
4 or 5 dashes Tabasco
1 tablespoon filé
1 to 2 quarts water
2 cans chicken broth

In a large pot over low heat place chicken broth, tomatoes with liquid, oyster liquid and about 1 cup water. When hot, stir in roux and gradually add enough water to make a thick broth. Add salt, pepper, and Tabasco and stir. Simmer covered for 30 minutes, stirring occasionally. Add shrimp, crab and oysters, and simmer for 30 minutes. Take off heat and stir in filé. Serve with a small helping of cooked rice. Serves 8-10. Recipe may be halved or doubled.

Chapter 5

You Can't Pick Up Spilled Milk

✳ ✳ ✳ ✳ ✳ ✳ ✳ ✳ ✳ ✳ ✳ ✳ ✳ ✳ ✳

It was one of those days when nothing seemed to go right. Ten people were scheduled to arrive at 6:30 for a dinner that just wasn't getting off the ground. When I left the house for a third trip to the supermarket to pick up yet another forgotten item, the soup was gently simmering on the stove. At least I thought so.

When I returned from the store, the pot was boiling vigorously and there was a terrible odor wafting through the kitchen. I quickly turned off the burner. "Maybe it only scorched the bottom of the pot and the rest of the cauldron will be okay." Wrong! After pouring the broth into another pot, there was no doubt that my beautiful creamy chowder had acquired the flavor of day-old burnt toast.

There was no saving the broth but, thank God, I hadn't put the shrimp in yet. There was still time to save the day. *How about a pasta dish?* Shrimp and feta cheese pasta sounded good and, luckily, there was enough feta cheese in the refrigerator. "Well, finally I have everything going pretty well," I said to myself.

You've heard of Murphy's Law: "If something can go wrong, it will." It did. As I poured out the soup, my hand slipped and the hot liquid cascaded down my arm. After I cleaned up the mess and put some salve on the burn, I hurried outside to put some meat on the grill. I had lit the barbecue earlier because I wanted the iron grid to be hot enough to score the lamb chops I had been marinating. When I reached the yard, with the plate of chops in hand, I discovered that there had only been enough gas in the tank to ignite the burners. The little bit of propane that remained had quickly burned itself out. For a moment I was tempted to cancel the whole thing. "I can call the guests, tell them I was burned and reschedule for another day." Just then, the adult side of my personality said, "What about the broiler? You can still prepare some mint and rosemary sauce and broiled lamb chops will work out fine."

Long story short, the guests ended up applauding the meal. They made numerous comments regarding the wonderful choice of menu and complimented Harriet and me on its preparation. When your carefully crafted plans go awry, sometimes all you can do is roll with the punches.

Life is often like that, dealing us surprises that we would never have wished for or expected. The fundamental truth is that we can't control what comes into our lives or the condition in which it arrives, but we can choose how we respond. To expect the world to be without problems is naïve and unrealistic. When we recognize and accept that life and people are just not perfect, we can learn to cope with the unexpected and adjust to the undesirable.

Carol never learned to cope or to adjust. Her mother was a remote, cold, unsupportive woman who had little to give to her children. She had gone through the motions of child rearing with her two older children, but by the time

Carol came along, her mother was totally drained emotionally. Carol was relegated to being cared for by her older sister, who resented the burden her baby sister represented. Because of this, she rejected Carol and left her with the feeling that her very existence caused problems and pain for others.

Her older brother was gone most of the time, and though she strongly admired him, he hardly noticed her. Her father was an enigma. He lived his life in virtual silence. He left for work before Carol awoke, came home in time for dinner, sat in his arm chair listening to the evening news on the radio, and went to bed early. This was the emotionally vacant home that Carol grew up in.

As she matured, Carol became increasingly adept at shutting the world out. She lived in a fantasy where things worked out well in the end and people lived happily ever after. She would occasionally snap back to reality with short bursts of anger, which she expressed through critical comments and caustic demands for love and emotional nurturing. Sadly, her mother was unable to respond, her father was too remote to even notice, and her siblings were so involved in their own emotional survival that they could hardly care. For the most part, Carol developed into a self-absorbed, desperately needy individual, who was too frightened to exert herself and too certain of rejection to risk asking for help.

She married a man who was as emotionally spent as her mother and as insecure as Carol herself. To make matters worse, when Carol was only forty-five years old, she was diagnosed with lupus. Her condition was both chronic and severe, which limited her physical activity and further reinforced her belief that she was a burden to others.

In spite of their emotional problems, Carol and Ronald were two very capable people intellectually.

Ronald's business acumen served him well and he advanced to an executive level in a large corporation. As his success increased at work, Ronald grew more confident and secure, both within himself and with others. As a result, he became increasingly dissatisfied with his home life.

Meanwhile, Carol became egocentrically preoccupied and consumed with her physical problems. She suffered constant emotional pain because her fairy-tale expectations were never satisfied. Victimized by her own contemplation and disappointments, she grew even more bitter toward others. The eventual outcome was a divorce brought on by her frequent venomous outbursts.

Nine years ago, Ronald accepted another promotion at work and transferred to the West Coast. There he met and married someone else. Carol continues to wallow in bitterness and anger, and she remains socially and emotionally estranged. She can ill afford to be otherwise. If she were to stop blaming others, she would have to face her own reality and accept the fact that her current plight is primarily her own doing.

Betsy grew up in a family steeped in a rigid Germanic cultural ethic. Monetary success and other material rewards of hard work and a no nonsense, non-emotional stoicism were all that mattered. Betsy's older brother worked with her parents in the family business and reaped the financial benefits. Her sister was beautiful and the apple of her father's eye, but she was also cold and selfish. She compensated for the lack of emotional nurturing in the home by manipulating her parents to gain as many material possessions as possible.

By contrast, Betsy was a sweet, good-natured daughter. She asked for nothing, caused no problems and hid any sign of emotional emptiness. Early on, the message she received was "Be good, be strong, be self-sufficient, and you will be loved." At a more basic level, the lesson she learned was, "Lie, hide, and deny who you really are. Suppress what you really feel and ignore what you really need, and others will love you."

Years later, she developed severe back problems that inhibited her ability to work or to care for her children and her home. In the midst of her pain, she convinced herself that she no longer loved her husband and asked him for a divorce. On the basis of her childhood experience, her behavior was easy to understand. In effect she was saying, "I can't afford to let you stop loving me because I can't perform, so I will stop loving you first." In other words, "You can't fire me—I quit!"

Richard came to therapy after years of living with a cold, emotionally unresponsive wife, who was similar in many respects to his mother. He had "hung in there" until their only child, a son, had graduated from high school and left for college. In therapy, he learned that if you want to alter your world, you have to start with yourself—you can't change someone else. He began to see that his actions over the first twenty years of his marriage were based on his ingrained expectation of rejection. The slightest hint of disapproval or distance from his wife was sufficient to justify his escape into work or sports. As far as he was concerned, he had already experienced all the rejection he could tolerate during childhood. His mother, whom he never met, left him in an orphanage, which later placed him with three or four sets of foster parents. No one ever chose to adopt him. At the age of eighteen, he moved out and in his own words, "I have been on my own ever since." When he finally learned that his foster care experience had nothing to do with his wife and present family, he was able to begin forging a new emotional life for himself by learning new responses to his old feelings.

Richard didn't cook, but he was able to understand what he had to do when he viewed life in the context of his favorite pastime and greatest love, baseball. Both marriage and baseball require that you get at least three strikes before you stop batting. (If you've ever been to the ballpark you know that as long as you can keep fouling the ball off, you can stay at the plate all night.) If you throw in the towel after one strike, you will never win the game and your marriage will never stand a chance. Richard also learned that he needed some new "batting techniques," as follows:

1. If you want to get a hit, lean into the ball, don't bail out of the box. In relationships, get involved if you want to improve your batting average. Don't bail out.

2. Stay balanced, with your feet planted firmly on the ground. Don't fly off into orbit or run away.

3. Timing is everything. If you swing too early or too late, you miss the ball. In a marriage, even a good thing said at the wrong time can elicit disastrous results.

4. Keep your eye focused on the ball. If you want to win at the game of marriage you must make the relationship your goal and focus on the ball. Don't make idle threats or abuse your spouse verbally, emotionally, or physically. And don't look for greener pastures. The Astroturf is just as hard in the other ballpark.

5. Baseball and marriage are team sports. You have to play with the other members of the team if you want to win. To become a team player, learn your partner's idiosyncrasies, understand his or her needs, and respect your differences.

Richard proved to be a wonderful student. He not only learned these rules, he applied them. The proof of the pudding (to get us back to the kitchen) is that both he and his wife agree that their twenty-year marriage is far better today than it was for the previous nineteen years.

Nine months ago, Richard came back to therapy after being diagnosed with cancer. At first, he reverted to the same coping strategies that had once hampered his marriage. He anticipated the worst, he was constantly on guard, he was in a continuous state of panic, and he wanted to run but didn't know where. He could not verbalize the C-word, and in his mind he frequently contemplated suicide. Today, Richard's panic is almost totally gone. He has no idea what the future holds as a result of his cancer, but he is back to living life to the fullest. He has openly acknowledged that he can't control the cancer but he can control his own emotional state and his behavioral reactions. He is actively involved with his wife, his son, and his friends. He is using his energy to live life, not fight it or succumb to it.

Obviously, the problems experienced by Carol, Betsy, and Richard are of far greater consequence than the pot of spoiled soup, the mild burn on my arm, and the "trauma" of having to serve broiled, versus grilled, lamb chops at my dinner party. Nevertheless, there is an important lesson to be learned from this parable. Mistakes in cooking and in life are not terminal. In the course of living, cheesecakes crack and soufflés fall, other people reject us or hurt us—or we reject or hurt them—but there are ways to correct our mistakes and turn them into victories.

So the broth is scalded, you've gotten burned, and there is no gas left in the barbecue. But that is all past. Turn your focus to what you still have in the cupboard. Maybe you need to look in the freezer. Either way, start with the ingredients you have. Every human being has value, creativity, and vision. It's part of being human. Remember the lessons that Richard learned: lean in, stay balanced, and focus your energy on living in the present.

Nobody has ever experienced a perfect upbringing. And nobody can change past hurts and scars. But we can adapt and we can move on. Character is born out of adversity. Don't spend the rest of your life trying to change the past; you can't pick up spilled milk. Instead, mop it up and pour yourself a fresh glass of positive, healthy living.

Salmon Chowder

Step one: don't burn the broth. With a little effort this dish will prove to be a crowd-pleaser at a dinner party or a wonderful starter for a romantic dinner for two on a winter's night. Best of all it doubles or triples easily and freezes well. You can make all kinds of heart-healthy substitutions without altering the taste. Try it, it is wonderfully satisfying.

5 cups milk (regular is preferable but I have on occasion used skim milk)
3 lbs. potatoes peeled and cut into 2" cubes
1 teaspoon sea salt or to taste
3 carrots peeled and sliced thin (a small package of frozen slices can be substituted)
8 oz. cream cheese (I have used low-fat cream cheese without adverse effect)
3 large onions minced
6 tablespoons butter or a butter substitute
1 to 1-1/2 lbs. salmon fillet, skinned and boned
1/2 teaspoon lemon pepper
3-1/2 tablespoons flour
4 tablespoons minced fresh dill (or 2 teaspoons dried)
3 to 4 large sprigs of fresh dill (for garnish)
2 tablespoons fresh lemon juice (microwave the lemon for 1 minute on medium heat before squeezing)

Combine the potatoes, carrots, salt and milk. Bring to a boil and simmer until vegetables are tender but not mushy, about 10 to 15 minutes. Meanwhile, in a large pot, sauté the onions in the butter over medium low heat until soft but not browned.

Lay the salmon fillet, cut in half if need be, on the onions, sprinkle generously with sea salt, lemon pepper and lemon juice. Place sprigs of dill over salmon or sprinkle with two teaspoons of dried dill; cover with a buttered round of wax paper and place lid on the pot. Cook for 8 to 10 minutes, turning once until the fillets are cooked but still firm to the touch. Remove salmon to a plate, sprinkle the flour over the onions and cook the mixture for 3 to 4 minutes, stirring constantly, until thickened. Add the milk mixture, including potatoes and carrots, along with cream cheese and whisk until smooth. Simmer for five minutes, stirring occasionally. Add salmon broken into chunks, mix in dill, and season to taste. Cook 5 to 10 minutes more over moderate heat until thoroughly heated. Garnish with fresh dill sprigs. Serves 4.

Chapter 6

Life's a Buffet

❋ ❋ ❋ ❋ ❋ ❋ ❋ ❋ ❋ ❋ ❋ ❋ ❋ ❋ ❋

When I think back to my childhood, one of the more memorable events was the first time a friend and I got to go downtown on our own. We planned the whole day, down to the last penny we would need for lunch, a movie and the essential boxes of Raisinettes and Good & Plenty. We rode the trolley to the center of Philadelphia and headed straight for the H & H Cafeteria. I remember walking wide-eyed down the buffet line, awestruck by the array of food. Making my selections was no easy task. When I finally reached the cash register, the cashier glanced at my tray, then looked at me rather peculiarly and said, "Are you sure that's what you want?" I had picked out mashed potatoes and gravy, french-fries, macaroni and cheese, and my favorite dessert at the time, pineapple cheese pie. Is it any surprise that I was a fat little fellow?

What I had on my tray was no accident. I had chosen the things that looked good to me. Perhaps the same can be said for all of us. Where we are in life, who we have become, and what we have accumulated, both tangibly and intangibly, is the result of the choices we have made. Some have chosen better than others.

That thought may be a difficult pill to swallow. After all, who wants to see themselves as a fat, lonely, poor, unsuccessful failure and have to admit it's of their own choosing? No one in their right mind would readily accept that notion. When I was a kid, if you had even mildly suggested that I wanted to be fat, I would have questioned the number of cards in your deck. I had no idea, at that young age, that I was feeding an empty stomach to fill an empty heart. Nevertheless, my being fat started out as a choice—a means of literally and figuratively covering my inner feelings of pain and loneliness.

The same principle applies to everyone. We all make significant choices that affect the course of our lives. Although we might attribute our situation to good or bad luck, or unforeseen circumstances, in truth we make deliberate decisions that contribute to where we end up.

To my way of thinking, life really is a buffet. We can't control which items we will encounter on the buffet of life, but we can decide which ones we put on our tray, how large a portion we are going to order and how much of it we are going to consume. The problem is rarely one of determining which choice to make. Instead, we struggle with making the choices that we already know are right for us.

Quite a few years ago, a group of psychologists conducted a survey to study the nature of love. They drew five test groups from radically differing backgrounds, social situations, and life experiences. Group one consisted of high school teenagers. Group two was composed of engaged couples in their twenties. The members of group three had all been married for thirty years or more. Everyone in group four had been divorced two or more times, and group five consisted of individuals in jail for sexual crimes and spousal abuse.

In all, hundreds of individuals were asked the question, "What is love?" The results, though initially surprising, were predictable. Everyone said essentially the same thing. In describing love, everyone used words like sharing, caring, communicating, trusting, closeness, talking, liking each other, having sexual feelings for, having good chemistry, being comfortable with each other, and having the same values, beliefs, and religious outlook.

What is significant is that their life experiences had apparently not affected their thoughts regarding the nature of love, and what they believed about love did not seem to affect what they did about it. Their choices in life were made on the basis of other factors.

Over the years, I have treated many psychotherapists, marriage counselors, ministers, psychologists and psychiatrists in therapy. Many were excellent counselors themselves, but when it came to their own problems, all their professional knowledge seemed of little consequence. Knowing what to do and doing what we know are radically different situations. When we're telling someone else, we make judgments based on our intellectual understanding. When we're choosing for ourselves, we make decisions out of our emotional being. Personal decisions are based primarily on feelings and attitudes we developed during our first seven or eight years of life and then habitualized as adults.

Often it seems we have two voices speaking inside of us. Sometimes they argue or try to drown each other out. One voice is shouting, "Have another piece of cheesecake," "Go ahead and smoke that cigarette," "Pour another round of drinks." Meanwhile the other voice says, "You don't need that cheesecake, you're trying to lose weight," "Forget the cigarette, you're already coughing up a storm," "Skip the drink, you still need to drive home." Unfortunately, we usually listen to the voice saying "Damn the torpedoes, full speed ahead."

If we are ever going to change this process we must learn how to take conscious charge of ourselves. Step one is learning to recognize both of the voices within us and deciding ahead of time which to heed or follow. Ask yourself, out loud if necessary, whether you are going to listen to what you know is best or let an emotional, impulsive eight-year-old make your decisions for you—that kid who places mashed potatoes and gravy, macaroni and cheese, and french-fries on the cafeteria tray.

He really isn't a bad little kid. He just needs some parental guidance. We are the only ones who can give him what he needs, because only we can speak directly to our inner child. The next time you find yourself face to face with a buffet consisting of a wide selection of emotions, don't choose a plate of misery, sadness or animosity. Instead, reach for a heaping serving of warm, nourishing love, a bowl of positive relationships and a glassful of good humor. Then ask someone to join you at your table.

Maybe you never realized you had a choice. You do. Life's a buffet and you're an adult. The emotions you choose to hold on to are what you will end up eating. Don't let the eight-year-old stuff your tray with junk.

Step two is mustering the courage to make a decision and running the risk of failure. What if you make a bad choice? Learn from your mistake and don't choose that stuff again. Occasionally, you're going to grab a dish that looks tasty but isn't. That's how you learn. The point is to make decisions based on informed, insightful, clear-headed thinking. Then the cashier on the buffet line of life will look at our tray and say, "Hey, good choice."

Gulf Coast Shrimp Buffet

This recipe is special. Cooking is easy—only takes one pot—and it's low in fat, which makes it great for weight-conscious individuals. It's a wonderful way to serve eight hungry people, but it can be doubled or tripled with ease if you have a large enough pot. How you serve it depends on your own style but one way is to cover your table with newspaper, put foil or freezer paper in the center of the table, drain the pot and pour all the food in the center of the table. Hand out paper plates, lots of melted butter, cocktail and rémoulade sauces, and let everyone dig in.

2 tablespoons salt
4 lemons, cut in half
3 heads of garlic
2 cans of beer
1 package crab boil
1/4 cup Tabasco sauce or to taste
16 small red potatoes scrubbed
8 small onions
8 ears of corn broken in half (fresh is preferable, but
     frozen will work)
2 lbs. of smoked spicy sausage such as kielbasa, etc.
1 head of cabbage quartered
4 lbs. of large shrimp

Fill a very large pot with water, bring to a boil and add the first six ingredients. You can squeeze lemons first if you prefer but don't bother doing a thing to the heads of garlic. Add the potatoes, cover and boil about 15 minutes. Add the onions and boil another 15 minutes. Add sausage cut into small chunks along with the corn and the chunks of cabbage (which I place in a mesh cloth boiling bag) and boil another 15 minutes. Then add the shrimp, cover and cook about three minutes. Time depends on the water temperature and how heavy a boil you have but when the shrimp begin to turn pink they are done. Nothing is worse than overcooked shrimp. Hint: the strained cooking water is wonderful for making a seafood gumbo and may be frozen for later use.

Chapter 7

Lemon Logic

✳ ✳ ✳ ✳ ✳ ✳ ✳ ✳ ✳ ✳ ✳ ✳ ✳ ✳ ✳

Pat is a forty-eight-year-old divorcee. Despite being an accomplished artist and a sharp salesperson who possesses a keen, intuitive understanding of others, her self-perception is that she is unworthy of love. Her feelings of intellectual insufficiency, self-doubt and lack of emotional worth result in efforts to avoid failure and rejection rather than seeking success.

Her childhood was deprived of emotional nurturing, physical warmth, or family support. She rarely dated in school and never felt comfortable in close interpersonal relationships. Her marriage ended when her husband decided to stop trying to live up to her emotional demands. Unfortunately, the only way she knew how to ask for love and attention was to find fault, complain, and lapse into depression.

Like a lemon that has been left in the freezer, Pat comes across as cold, hard and sour. She sees herself as desperately needing "juice," but not being able to give it.

Brad is at the opposite end of the spectrum. An attorney, he lives by the maxim that the best defense is a strong offense. When pressured, he is likely to explode like a lemon microwaved on high heat. During our initial appointment, I asked him why he needed a defense in the first place. The answer was obvious when I heard his story.

When Brad was eight years old, his mother died. He was sent to live with his grandmother, but she died two years later. In the meantime, his father married a woman who totally rejected Brad. As a result, he was sent to live with an aunt, whose husband later divorced her. She went into a major depression and had to give Brad up to other relatives. His life became a series of short-lived stays in different homes. No wonder he is reluctant to trust another person in a relationship. In his mind, he desperately wants love, a family, and a home, but in his heart he cannot believe it will ever happen. Consequently, whenever he begins to care for someone, he ends up pushing them away to avoid the rejection he knows will eventually occur. He is driven by the emotional certainty that history will always repeat itself. Because of his need to protect himself emotionally, his adult life has been a long trail of broken hearts.

Debbie is an entrepreneur who gives off an air of professional confidence and assertiveness. During her first visit, she said, "All my life I paid little attention to men or dating. I concentrated on my career. Now, at thirty-eight, I'm interested, but the only guys I attract are weak creeps. All they want is for me to take care of them."

Is it an accident or a coincidence that she draws this type of man? I deduced that she probably had never thought of herself as worthy of being cared for. I surmised that something in her childhood contributed to her inability to trust others and to her primary drive to be financially and emotionally self-sufficient. When I heard her story, I discovered that her father had betrayed her when she was young and her mother had done nothing to protect her. How could she possibly trust that anyone would ever be there for her?

Now, as an adult, she feels drained of all of her emotional juice, and she is wary of trusting emotions from others. She can neither give nor receive love freely.

All three of these patients have at least one thing in common. They all think something is wrong with them. Pat knows that something is wrong with her or her parents would not have treated her with such disdain and distance. Brad is convinced that there must be something severely lacking in him to cause his mother, grandmother, father, stepmother, and aunt to abandon him. Debbie feels either totally empty or filled with guilt and shame. She is certain that something about her is evil and unworthy of love.

These common feelings of emotional insufficiency limit the extent to which these three individuals are able to participate in intimate, meaningful relationships. Unfortunately, most individuals experience some feelings of inadequacy. We all experience a loss in our sense of self-worth equivalent to the degree that we have been hurt or deprived. The only difference between my patients and everyone else is the amount of emotional hurt and the degree of conscious awareness.

Sadly but truly, few of us ever exceed the limits of our sense of self-sufficiency. Thus, if we believe, even unconsciously, that we can't make it in college, we're right, we won't. If we believe that we will never reach management level at work, there is no doubt we'll be correct. Most of us tend to actualize our greatest fears. If we believe that anyone we love will ultimately reject us, hurt us, or betray us, we will undoubtedly be drawn to people who will ensure that very outcome.

However, there is a positive side. Think about it this way: If a negative sense of self-worth results in negative relationships, it should be equally true that positive feelings toward ourselves will result in positive, healthy relationships.

There's only one problem. We need to learn how to enhance the way we feel and behave toward ourselves. Of course, it's only a problem until we discover that, like the average lemon, there is more "juice" in each and every one of us than we ever realized. We have more to give to ourselves and more to share with others than we have ever begun to tap.

Have you ever used a recipe that called for "the juice of one lemon?" Exactly how much juice is that? Perhaps when you squeezed the lemon you didn't get much juice. Well, I have a secret technique that will extract the maximum amount of juice that can possibly come from one lemon. And it's easy. Simply put the lemon in the microwave for one minute on medium heat. You will be amazed. When you cut the lemon in half, the juice will run out of its own accord. Try it!

If you had put that same lemon in the freezer overnight and then taken it out, you could hardly have cut it in half, let alone expected it to provide any juice. Conversely, if you had put it into the microwave on high heat for two or three minutes, it would have exploded and you would have had a terrible mess. Well, it's the same way with people. If we approach them with heated emotions and a hot temper, the likelihood is they will respond in a similar fashion. They will explode and we will have a terrible mess. On the other hand, if we approach them with an air of cool indifference or give them the cold shoulder, we can be certain they will respond in an equally frigid manner. The end result will be no juice, no closeness of any kind. But if we approach other people with the right degree of warmth, without being saccharine or seductive, we will elicit feelings that will be soothing to our hearts.

The lesson we learn from a lemon is the same as the Golden Rule: "Do unto others as you would have them do unto you." We've heard this maxim repeated ever since we were children, yet very few of us follow this principle in our dealings with others. Unfortunately, we often save our worst behavior for those who mean the most or those whose love we want the most.

The principle of "do unto others" works like priming a pump. Maybe that's our problem. Few of us grew up with an old fashioned pump that required priming. In the old days, if you wanted water from the well, you first had to pour water down the pump to eliminate the trapped air and create suction, thereby enabling the pump to bring the water to the surface. Relationships essentially work the same way. What you pour in is what you get out in greater measure.

The reason most of us don't practice the simple principle of priming the pump is that we fail to realize how much "emotional juice" we have to put in. Despite our best outward appearances, we frequently are unconsciously defensive or closed down emotionally, and therefore feel reluctant or incapable of genuinely sharing our feelings. After all, how can we possibly give to someone else what we don't possess ourselves? Like the gently warmed lemon, there's more juice inside us than we realize

To discover the wealth of our own personal value, we must begin to approach ourselves with more self-awareness, more self-acceptance, more forgiveness, more warmth and more kindness than ever before. As we take these steps, our feelings of passion and warmth will literally flow from within us of their own accord. If it works for lemons, why not warm up to the possibility that it can work for you?

Lemon Pasta

This is an easy dish that you can't mess up. Similar to almost every recipe in the book, you can modify it according to your taste. You can make it thick or thin depending on how much pasta water or Parmesan cheese you add. The lemon taste can be increased by adding more lemon juice and/or lemon peel. This dish goes well with meat, chicken or fish but can stand on its own as a pasta course. The original recipe called for linguine, but on one occasion I discovered I had none so I substituted Farfalle. Everyone raved about it. From that moment on, the pasta shape for this dish—at least in my home—was changed forever.

1 lb. linguine or Farfalle (bowtie noodles)
1 cup reserved pasta cooking water
1 teaspoon minced garlic
1 cup whipping cream
4 tablespoons butter
2 tablespoons lemon peel
6 tablespoons fresh lemon juice
1 cup Parmesan cheese
2 tablespoons chopped Italian parsley
 salt and pepper to taste
8 thin lemon slices

While the pasta water is boiling, bring the cream and butter to a simmer in a large skillet over medium to medium-high heat. Add the garlic, lemon juice and lemon peel. By then the pasta water will have come to a rolling boil, and you can add some salt if you prefer (water boils faster without salt so adding it at the end is a time-saving technique). Cook the pasta until *al dente* or firm to the bite. Drain the pasta, but remember to save a cup or more of pasta water. Add the pasta to the cream mixture. Toss, adding the cheese, Italian parsley, salt and pepper. If you prefer a thinner consistency (I usually do), add reserved pasta water as desired. Garnish with additional Parmesan cheese, a sprig of parsley and a thin lemon slice. Serves 8.

Chapter 8

Cottage Cheese Therapy

✻ ✻ ✻ ✻ ✻ ✻ ✻ ✻ ✻ ✻ ✻ ✻ ✻ ✻ ✻

The engineer nodded and I switched on the mike. The ON AIR sign lit and I started my usual introduction: "Hi, I'm Dr. Ed Reitman and this is the Dr. Ed Show. I will be taking your calls for the next three hours with the hope that I can help make your life just a little bit better. There are several lines open and if you dial right now, your call will be one of the first on the air after a short break for news and weather." I switched off the mike and leaned back in my chair. Things could not have been much better. Only two days earlier, the *Houston Post* had run an article titled "Dr. Ed Show Beats Out Monday Night Football." The new issue of the Southwest Airlines in-flight magazine had a four-page article about me, including a full-page photograph. The phones were ringing off the wall and the feedback I was getting was wonderful. Perhaps I should have known better. Sometimes, euphoria doesn't last long.

The door to the broadcast room opened and the station manager entered. He had his own news. It was short and to the point. Monday Night Football, Rockets basketball and

Sports Beat were far more profitable than I was. He told me to finish the present show and say my goodbyes the following evening. My stomach dropped like an elevator from the top of a fifty-story building. My mind raced through various options for how to respond. I could go out in a blaze of glory (I won't spell that one out); I could plead for listeners to call the station demanding that I stay on the air; I could expose the world's lack of concern for people and how business is ruled by Profit and Loss statements; or I could handle it like a professional, expressing gratitude for my two years on the air, and offering the listeners my good wishes and hopes that their lives were a little bit better as a result of the time we had spent together. Fortunately, common sense ruled.

On the positive side—if there is a positive side to being dumped—the station had resolved a problem that I anticipated having with my wife. Barely a week earlier, she had come through loud and clear with her pronouncement that "you might be doing wonders for the rest of Houston by leaving the house seven days a week at 6:30 a.m. and returning home each night at 11:00 p.m. after three hours on the air, but you're not helping your kids, your wife, or your marriage." Recognizing the truth in her statement, I promised to rectify the situation by the first of the year, which gave me ninety days to either appease her, change me, or alter my situation. Then, in one fell swoop, it was all resolved.

The entire interaction with the station manager took only a matter of seconds. The news was still on so I had time to make a call. I lifted the phone and dialed my home number.

"You will never guess what just happened," I told my wife in a rather depressed fashion. Before I could finish the sentence, I heard her elated response.

"They fired you!" Her voice seemed filled with glee. "That's wonderful! I'll stay up and make a special meal. What do you want?"

I was aghast. How could she be so insensitive? Before I could say another word, she said, "I know you feel bad and I really am sorry, but it really is great. We'll be able to have evenings together. You will be less pressured...I am happy about it all. Now, tell me, what can I make for you?"

"Nothing," I answered. "I don't want a thing. I've gotta go. The news is almost over."

As far as I was concerned, she should have known that if I wasn't hungry, I must be in a bad way. After all, wasn't she the one who always said, "You are the only person I know who eats even when he is sick." Of course she knew that I was upset, but she also knew that the best gift she could give me was the gift of my own reality. She had heard me say it a million times, and now my words were coming home to roost.

Three hours later, I left the station and drove home to a dark house. Harriet was sound asleep, or at least appeared to be, which was appropriate because she teaches mentally disabled children in a public middle school and she needs her rest. Following my customary routine, I went to the kitchen, where I found nothing but clean counters. I opened the refrigerator. Nothing. I opened the microwave and then the oven. Both were empty. In desperation, I searched for my one standby—cottage cheese—but the refrigerator was still bare.

That was the last straw. I stormed into the bedroom, awakened my wife and enumerated my grievances:

1. Didn't she know how bad I felt? (In other words, wasn't I irritable enough?)

2.   She hadn't made me any dinner. (Of course, she had offered, but I had refused it.)

3.   She hadn't waited up. (Who in her right mind would wait up to greet an angry bear?)

4.   There was no cottage cheese. (For a man who is constantly on a diet, not having cottage cheese is an unpardonable sin.)

I followed up my initial tirade with speech number 394a: "How can a person diet when he gets no help? I'm out working from 6 a.m. to 11 at night and you can't even buy cottage cheese." Harriet simply rolled her eyes as she turned over to go back to sleep. (My son-in-law informs me that my daughter executes this maneuver with the same degree of effectiveness.)

I went to bed a starving martyr. The next morning, I left before Harriet awoke. That evening, following my last show, I came home to the same dark house and the same sleeping wife. In the kitchen, I found the same clean counters, and the same empty microwave and oven.

Then I opened the refrigerator. Every shelf was filled to capacity with large cartons of cottage cheese. I tried my best to be angry. But try as I might, I couldn't help but smile. No words were ever so eloquent as twenty-eight tubs of cottage cheese.

Harriet understood my loss and she had tried to console me, but I would have none of it. She had tried to celebrate the positive, but I wouldn't allow that either. I was too busily engaged in feeling sorry for myself and I was determined to suffer. And if others were made to suffer along with me, so much the better.

Finally, Harriet gave me the gift of my own reality. She had the courage to be honest, to hold the mirror up in front of me and say, "Look at yourself, 'Don Quixote.'

That's a spittoon on your head, a bag-of-bones horse between your legs, and you've been fighting windmills." She accomplished her purpose with love, humor, kindness and courage.

The gift of someone's reality is the most important gift you can give to your spouse, your children, or your friends. At the same time, it is probably the most difficult gift to give as well. Most of us are reluctant to look at our reality: the motivating factors behind the things we say, the things we do, the feelings we have and the attitudes we project. Consequently, these motivating factors—our reality—are often invisible to us. It is always easier to point the finger at someone else and to blame them for our upset feelings, the stress we feel, or even the inappropriate behaviors we demonstrate.

The problem is, without an awareness of our own reality, change or growth never occurs. To grow, we first have to believe that there is something we can modify or change. When we point our finger at someone else, when we view ourselves as the victim, emotional growth never occurs, because instead of taking ownership of ourselves, our attitudes and our actions, we are saying that the problem belongs to someone else. That's why it is helpful—even essential—to have a partner, a friend, or a spouse who is courageous enough and cares enough to risk our initial defensive reaction and give us the gift of our own reality.

One of the things I most appreciate about my wife is her courage to be honest with me in spite of my all-too-frequent initial anger, defensiveness or retaliatory responses. Fortunately, Harriet isn't afraid of me; if she were, the gift of my reality would never be in her repertoire.

To give your loved ones the gift of their own reality, you face your own fears and act in spite of them, not because of them. You must risk the possibility of being rejected by someone you love in order to help them see who they are and where they are coming from.

Too often, we try to deliver the "gift" during an argument or when we're angry. Unfortunately, anger is like wrapping paper that says "I've been meaning to tell you this for a long time and I'm going to get it off my chest right now." From my own experience, any "gift" given to me wrapped in anger is not appreciated. Instead, I receive it with fear and defensiveness, and I don't see it as a gift at all. I see it as a time for fight or flight. Even under the best of circumstances, I need to be sufficiently brave, comfortable and emotionally secure to be able to receive the gift of my own reality in an open and loving fashion. Rarely does one say, "Thanks for showing me how I really am," even when it comes wrapped in soft, loving words.

Reality is a powerful gift. Timing, humor, and genuine care can make the bitter pill of our own reality easier to swallow. In giving this gift, we hope that the seeds of our words fall on fertile soil and will bear fruit in the future. In the meantime, the giver of the gift must be aware that helping someone to see themselves can on occasion be a hurtful, thankless task. It takes great courage to give the gift of reality, and it often takes even more courage to accept it. After all, twenty-eight cartons of cottage cheese can be hard to swallow.

Harriet's Noodle Pudding or Kugel

This is one of my favorite recipes that uses cottage cheese. It is another easy but delicious dish that can accompany a roast or brisket or can be served on a buffet.

1 lb. wide egg noodles
1 pint sour cream
1 pint cottage cheese
1 cup milk
1 cup yellow raisins
2 teaspoons nutmeg
2 teaspoons salt
4 tablespoons sugar
6 tablespoons melted butter
1/4 teaspoon cinnamon
crushed cornflakes

Cook the noodles according to the directions on the package; drain and rinse with cold water. In a large bowl mix the other ingredients, add the noodles and mix thoroughly. Place the mixture in a large, greased glass casserole and top with slightly crushed cornflakes and dot with lots of butter. At this point it can be frozen, refrigerated for baking the next day or baked immediately. Start with the casserole dish at room temperature. Preheat oven to 375° and bake for 1-1/2 hours. Serves 8.

Chapter 9

Don't Let Stuff Stew

⁂ ⁂ ⁂ ⁂ ⁂ ⁂ ⁂ ⁂ ⁂ ⁂ ⁂ ⁂ ⁂ ⁂ ⁂

There is nothing like a plate of hot beef stew on a cold winter night. Think of it. Tender chunks of meat in a rich, brown gravy with potatoes, carrots, onions, celery, mushrooms, and a blend of spices, served with hot, crusty bread and melted butter. There's a meal that is so-o-o-o satisfying to the stomach. Add some red wine and herbs of Provence to the ingredients and it becomes beef Bourguignonne, a dish fit for a French king. Set the table in front of the fireplace, with candlelight, soft music and champagne, and the meal is transformed into a romantic evening that warms the soul.

But if you cook the stew too long, the ingredients break down and you wind up with a mishmash or hash that under the best of circumstances would never grace a royal table or serve as the main entrée for a romantic dinner for two. The ingredients lose their distinction and the resulting flavor lacks character.

Sometimes we keep ourselves in a stew. We take old hurts, old wounds, and old pains and keep them simmering inside on low heat. Eventually, these hurts and pains permeate into every facet of life, contaminating our relationships and undermining our emotional well-being. They may, over time, lapse from our consciousness, but the feelings they evoke are still simmering. Days, weeks, or even months later, we recall, at a subconscious level, the old resentments and the anger we felt. Because of these feelings, we maintain a physical or emotional distance from others. Ironically, if we tried to recall the specific facts or details of the original controversy, we would likely discover we stewed so long that the ingredients have long since lost their identity. Nevertheless, the hurt and the pain are still there, a tasteless mishmash of negative emotions. Worse yet, they undermine our significant relationships.

The solution is to empty the pot, learn from our errors, and start over with the same meat and potatoes. Remember, the main ingredients are not at fault; it's how they were prepared or how long they cooked that caused the problem. Likewise, the significant others in our lives are not the problem, but the way we interact or respond makes all the difference.

When Helen first came into my office, she spent the first forty minutes of a fifty-minute session listing her husband's faults. Finally she said, "I will never forgive Richard for what he did when little Charlie was born. He was out on that oil rig in the Gulf and my mother called and told him I was going to the hospital, but he never got there until three hours after little Charlie was born."

I'm certain she would have continued her litany for the remainder of the session had I not interrupted with a question. "How old is little Charlie now?"

Without missing a beat she answered, "Thirty-five years old."

I know that my mouth momentarily dropped open in sheer amazement. "Thirty-five?" I said in disbelief.

"Yes" she said, without a trace of irony.

"That's a long time to be unforgiving, isn't it?" I said gently.

She stopped for a moment as though genuinely considering my question. "Yes," she said hesitantly, in an almost embarrassed tone.

Georgeann found herself in almost the same situation. She and Sid were in a joint session when she suddenly whipped out a sheaf of typed pages, one for every month of the previous year. By date she had listed the number of times he had played tennis, gone hunting or fishing, or been up at the deer lease "with the boys" fixing up the place or scouting trails so they would know where to set up the deer stands next season. It was a grievous list that totally invalidated his statement from the week before that he was hardly ever gone.

She had more than proven her point, but she was left speechless by his retort. He said, "I admit I was wrong but I am flabbergasted that you and your secretary kept tabs on me for more than a year and that the two of you took all that time to compile and type these negative behavioral accounts. What bothers me even more is that you never once made note of the couple dozen times I sent you flowers, the surprise gifts I gave you, the notes I wrote or the evenings we stayed home having dinner in bed and watching movies we had rented. What were you trying to do? Improve our marriage or find grounds for a divorce?"

Both Georgeann and Helen absolutely told the truth. Neither is crazy or out of touch with reality. Georgeann's list is a testimony to a years worth of factual documentation. Helen's forty minutes of uninterrupted grievances add up to thirty-five years of differences and distance. The sad thing is that Georgeann and Helen aren't alone. Without conscious awareness, many of us go through life investing our time, our emotions and our energy in endeavors guaranteed to produce negative results, elicit negative feelings, and cause estrangement between us and those we claim to love—and the very people we want to love us. We act like IRS agents who are rewarded by promotions and awards for finding fault and prosecuting offenders. The payoff for the IRS agent is obvious. The payoff for the rest of us is far more difficult to discern.

Here's an example that illustrates my point and exposes the hidden agenda involved. The Clark's first came to my office because of sexual problems. Lilly confessed, with some pride, that she has "always had a much stronger sexual appetite than Stephen. He is a kind, loving man but his sexual desires just don't match up with mine. That was all right with me until four months ago, when he entirely lost interest in sex. Doctor, if this can't be fixed, I don't know what I am going to do. I love him, but he can't expect me to 'do without' for the rest of my life."

Stephen admitted that sex wasn't a top priority in his life and that the more she complained, the less he gave a damn. Two weeks later, Lilly left town with several girlfriends to go to a spa in California. On Saturday morning, she called home and Stephen told her about his plans. He was going to drive out to his parent's house, pick up his father and brother, drive back to a ballpark near Stephen and Lilly's home, return to Mom and Dad's for dinner, and then drive home.

Without a moment's hesitation, Lilly pointed out that he would be making the same trip four times. In her opinion, it seemed far more economic in terms of time, gas, wear and tear on the car, and energy, if Dad and brother would drive to the ballpark and pick Stephen up on the way. They could swing by the house after the game so he could get his car to drive out to Mom and Dad's for dinner. "You see," she explained, "that will make two trips for you instead of four." She was absolutely correct if his primary purpose was to be economical.

Stephen came for his counseling appointment two days after the ball game. As a result of his conversation with Lilly, he had taken her suggestion and had altered his plans. It sounds fairly simple, but it isn't.

Stephen explained that he had really wanted to spend time with his father. His brother lived closer to their parents and was able to spend considerably more time with them than Stephen could. Driving to and from the ballpark and the time spent at the game was a rare opportunity to be together.

"If that is so," I questioned, "why did you change your plans?"

At first, Stephen said he wasn't sure, but later he implied that it just wasn't worth the flak he might receive from Lilly.

"Does that bother you?" I asked.

"It kind of bugs me. Here she is in California doing her thing, but she needs to call me to tell me what I should be doing here."

"What I hear you saying is that it did bother you, but it wasn't worth making waves. Let's consider another possibility. What about the idea that you want to be mad? Before you answer, I want you to know something. I think that, for you, staying mad is better than not getting mad at all. It's an improvement over mealy-mouthed statements like 'It kind of bugged me.' You are a master of understatement. It's almost as though you have never had permission to get mad at anyone except through passive-aggressive behavior. Is it possible that you are finally tired of feeling controlled and of not exercising your right to do what you truly want to do? Perhaps now you can go one step further by recognizing your own feelings, learning to express them without anger, and then no longer needing to hurt or deprive yourself in order to punish those you love."

"I don't understand," he responded.

"It just seems to me," I said, "that not having sex is a terrible price to pay in order to hurt someone else. Perhaps you need to consider that you have the right, even the responsibility, to express your own wishes, desires, and feelings, and to make choices without hurting yourself. You have got to stop stewing over old anger. Your behavior only cheats you and destroys any chance of your ever experiencing a healthy, loving relationship."

To really understand the three individuals in these examples, it is essential to examine their early years to see what has been cooking ever since their childhood.

Helen was sexually abused as a girl. Her early relationships with men were all hurtful and emotionally disappointing. Her marriage to Richard came about, in her mind, only as a result of a surprise and unwanted pregnancy. To this day, she still doubts that he ever cared for her. Her years of resentment over "little Charlie" are the defense she clings to in order to protect herself from present-day hurts. In essence, her theme might be, "You can't fire me; I quit thirty-five years ago."

Georgeann never felt she measured up. No matter what she accomplished, it never elicited the love she desperately wanted from her parents. She could never be a substitute for the son she felt her father desired, and her tomboyish behavior was a disappointment to her emotionally insecure mother. Consequently, she came to expect the same reactions from anyone she loves, and she fears the loving relationships she longs for. "A long list of rejections" enables her to justify restricting her emotional involvement. It also helps to minimize her caring too deeply and then being deeply hurt.

Stephen was raised by an extremely cold, controlling mother who dominated her husband and her children. Love was given conditionally and any display of demonstrative emotion was discouraged. Early on, he learned to play the game well. As a result, he became mother's favorite "little man." It is no surprise that years later he would behave the same way in his marriage. He has learned that controversy "isn't worth the hassle." He has also learned that the price for love is to sell yourself short.

In all three cases, the pot has been stewing far too long. Helen, Georgeann and Stephen have lost their identities. Their behavior is not synonymous with their inner feelings. They behave out of habits they learned as children. Any reflection of their true emotions and feelings have long since disappeared. They have made hash out of themselves, not beef Bourguignonne. They need to start again, to make themselves fit for a royal feast or, more importantly, a romantic lifetime for two.

The recipe is simple, though in real life it is not always easy to prepare. The first step is to recognize the worth of your own basic ingredients. The next step is to add new spices, like honesty, sentimentality and vulnerability, that perhaps you've never tried before. Then simmer slowly over a low emotional heat until the flavors blend into a tasty combination.

It should be noted that when you start to cook a new dish, the people around you might resist your efforts. We all tend to cling to the status quo. Your spouse may want you to stay the way you were when you first met or married. Even if the stew has lost its distinctive flavor, at least the hash tastes familiar. Often we choose the predictable over the fresh and the new, because if our partner changes, in many ways it obligates us to change as well.

But what is life without adaptation and change? The world is not a static place, and refusing to change means choosing to be left behind. Of course, I don't counsel my patients to leave their parents, family, partner or friends behind. I tell them to run toward what they fear—the possible rejection or potential pain—and say, "This is who I am. You can resist me or reject me but you can't make me stop loving you or caring for you."

Discard the mushy mess of overcooked resentments, fears, and failures and cook up a fresh perspective. Then set the table in front of the fireplace, light some candles, pop the cork on a bottle of champagne and serve this tasty new dish—you!—to someone you love. I promise that this recipe will nourish your heart and nurture your soul.

Beef Stew

This is one time that we want to let things stew. In fact I like to prepare this stew the day before and refrigerate it overnight. Before adding the finishing touches the following day, skim off most of the solidified fat that accumulates on the surface. It may seem as though there are a large number of ingredients, but almost all are items you already have in your kitchen. Don't be intimidated, this is a wonderful dish made in a large pot or roasting pan and will feed a hungry crowd. Serve with warm french bread that can be used for dipping, a large fresh salad, and a couple of bottles of red wine and you will be the host of a memorable party.

4 lbs. lean beef cubes
1 cup flour
seasoned salt and pepper to taste
4 tablespoons oil
4 tablespoons butter
3 large onions in 1/4 inch slices
1 pound mushroom quarters
4 garlic cloves minced
2 cans beer
2 cans beef broth
1/4 cup minced parsley
2 tablespoons light brown sugar
2 bay leaves
1 teaspoon dried thyme
2 teaspoons dried oregano
4 plum tomatoes diced
1 teaspoon salt
2 teaspoons pepper

6 carrots cut into 1/2 inch pieces
6 stalks celery cut into 1/2 inch pieces
2 lbs. new potatoes washed and quartered
1 large turnip in eight chunks
large pinch nutmeg
2 tablespoons red wine vinegar
1 teaspoon Kitchen Bouquet
1 teaspoon Worcestershire sauce

Mix flour, salt and pepper in a large bowl, add the beef cubes and toss to coat. (You can buy 4 pounds of trimmed and cubed stew meat or you can buy a 5 pound chuck roast, 2 to 3 inches thick, and trim and cube it yourself.) Melt the butter and oil in a heavy skillet over high heat. Sauté the beef in small batches and brown thoroughly.

Remove meat to a large heavy roasting pan. Add the onions to the skillet and brown lightly. Add quartered mushrooms and garlic, continue to brown over moderately high heat for about 5 more minutes. Transfer the contents of the skillet to the roasting pan. De-glaze the skillet with one can of beer; add beer with the browned bits from the bottom of the skillet to the meat, onions and mushrooms. Now add the remaining beer and beef broth to the meat mixture along with the parsley, brown sugar, bay leaves, thyme, oregano, tomatoes, and salt and pepper.

Cover and bring to a simmer on the top of the stove, add the nutmeg, vinegar, Kitchen Bouquet and Worcestershire sauce. Remove to a preheated 300° oven and bake 3 hours. Melt 1 tablespoon each of butter and oil in the same skillet and sauté the carrots and celery until slightly browned, about 5 minutes. Set aside and add to stew the last hour.

Periodically check meat to determine when it has reached a desired degree of tenderness. If the gravy is too thin, thicken with a mixture of 2 tablespoons cold water and 1 tablespoon of flour. If the gravy is too thick, thin with additional beef broth. Adjust flavoring with additional spices, or if it suits your taste, add several drops of Tabasco or other hot sauce. Serves 10.

Chapter 10

Too Much Sauce

❋ ❋ ❋ ❋ ❋ ❋ ❋ ❋ ❋ ❋ ❋ ❋ ❋ ❋ ❋

Harriet and I spent almost three weeks in France several summers ago. We rented a car, circumvented Paris and drove more than 2,300 miles. We made no reservations and had only a general notion of where we were going. The only thing we knew for certain was the date and time of our scheduled flight home from Charles DeGaulle Airport.

It was a glorious trip. Everywhere we went, the people were absolutely wonderful. Our total lack of knowledge of the language proved no problem. We stayed in inexpensive hotels that were quaint, clean, and comfortable. The bistro food was comforting to the stomach and tasted good. We truly had no disappointing experiences until we treated ourselves to a four-star restaurant toward the end of our trip. The meal, though artistically pleasing, was catastrophic to our pocketbook, meager in quantity, and lacking in quality. Most of the food was half-cooked or raw and the sauce, which was abundantly supplied, did little to disguise these deficiencies.

One morning over coffee and croissants at a small cafe, I expressed these thoughts to a Frenchman who was eagerly practicing his English on me. His explanation, whether accurate or not, seemed reasonable to me. During the Middle Ages, he said, fresh meat was available but refrigeration was only a gleam in the eye of an inventor yet to be born. Consequently, meat was often cooked and served despite the fact that it was old or on the verge of spoiling. Elaborate sauces were created to obscure the less-than-perfect taste. With the advent of refrigeration, the spoilage stopped, but the tradition of French sauces continued.

It is the same for people. All of us go through life creating sauces to cover up what we perceive to be lacking or unacceptable in ourselves. Some people get sauced literally, drinking themselves into oblivion. In other cases, the sauce directly compensates for a deficit we wish to obscure. For example, someone who feels emotionally insignificant or insufficient might become a braggart or a name dropper. Still others with a poor sense of self-worth become careless with the truth. As a result, much of what they tell you can be divided by three. For them, what they do, where they go, and what they have is always the best, the most important, or the only one of its kind. On the opposite end of the spectrum, many individuals attempt to hide their feelings of inadequacy by saying little, taking few risks, and only speaking up when they are totally confident of their responses.

Still others concoct elaborate sauces from ingredients such as beer, drugs, golf, tennis, video games, work, hypochondria, perfectionism, depression and anger. No matter what kind of sauce it is, the amount a person serves is equal to or greater than the degree to which he believes himself to be unacceptable or lacking. When people respond out of inner feelings of inadequacy, their sauce is all too readily available to be dished out.

Behavioral sauces are easy to recognize because they rarely change. After simmering inside for years, the same stories, the same behaviors and attitudes, bubble to the surface. They become a routine more than a reaction. "Here it comes again."

The strange thing about a chronic behavioral sauce is that, in most instances, it is blatantly apparent to others yet invisible to the person dispensing it. Of course, that is exactly how sauces are designed to work. The most effective sauces share two key characteristics. First, they mitigate or obscure hurtful feelings of insufficiency, fear, or inadequacy. And secondly, they become palatable to their creators, who come to view them as positively enhancing, protective of self, and equally palatable to others.

The best example I can give you is personal. From the time I was a youngster, I had three sauces, Fast, Funny, and Fat, any one of which I could serve up at a moment's notice.

I served up Fast Sauce in a furious flurry of activity. I was a whirling dervish who had five or six things going at any given time without being consciously aware. I thought the impression I was making was that of a hard-working, highly productive individual. All the while, I had a built-in excuse for not completing things or for finding another involvement whenever I felt failure was imminent.

I could dish out Funny Sauce without even thinking. Often at my own expense. As a kid, I had a little black book filled with punch lines from jokes, alphabetized by subject matter. I was never at a loss for a quip and humor concealed how bad I felt about myself. Jokes became a hiding place;

they should have been a neon sign blinking "Ed, you're not feeling good about yourself."

One incident stands out as an embarrassing example that I will remember for the rest of my life. I had just started a private practice in Houston. I was poor as a church mouse and very impressed (a polite way of saying "extremely intimidated") by the doctors' parking lot at the hospital. I frequently chose to park my four-and-a-half year old Nash Rambler station wagon behind my office. I would then walk across the street to the hospital, passing the array of Cadillacs, Lincolns, Mercedes, and Porsches owned by the "real" doctors. I typically entered the hospital through the emergency room and stopped by the doctors' lounge to visit, to establish new relationships, and to remind the other doctors that I was available for referrals.

On this particular day, I sat next to a surgeon I had met on several previous occasions but whom I hadn't seen for the past two or three weeks. I mentioned that I had missed him and wondered where he had been. He said, "I took my family to Europe." I responded with a joke about a doctor and his secretary. The surgeon laughed appropriately and then said casually, "I picked up a new Mercedes over in Europe. We toured around for awhile and then I shipped it back home. It should arrive in about two or three weeks. You will have to see it. It is a honey."

Again I countered with a funny story, this time about a guy with headaches who goes to an internist. The surgeon laughed as he stood up and said, "Well, I've got to go see a patient I just operated on. By the way, I have a referral I would like to give you. I'll call you when I get to the office. Also, if you and your family are not busy next weekend, I would love for you all to join us up at the ranch for a barbecue we are giving."

As he hurried out the door, I could hear a small voice inside me saying, "But I haven't told you the one about the farmer's daughter who..." To this day, I know in my soul that the last joke would never have topped the ranch and the invitation. You see, no amount of humor can cover up what you don't feel or can't accept inside yourself.

By the same token, food can never fill the empty feeling inside. Trust me, I served Fat Sauce for a lot of years. But no matter how much I ate, my relief was only short lived. I no longer felt bad on the inside, but the outside was horrendous. I hated the results. Every time I looked in the mirror, my self-perception diminished. I was a self-propelled perpetual emotion machine. I couldn't tell that I was feeling insecure, inadequate, or insufficient. Consciously, I only knew that I was hungry so I ate to satisfy the hunger. Before long, I no longer felt the need for food, but I hated my body image so I ate even more. Strangely enough, it seemed easier to hate my outside than to deal with what was going on inside. I became so consumed by the entire process that I never had to confront what I was really feeling. The Fat Sauce worked well. I never smelled whatever it was that tasted bad inside.

Today I am not half as fat, half as frantic, or half as funny as I used to be, but I am five times happier and five times more content with who I am. The cure wasn't like a light switch—one minute dark, the next minute shining light—it was more a case of three steps forward, two steps back, but it worked. Of course, I still occasionally feel the need for a serving of sauce, but more often than not, I catch myself and say, "Ed, it is okay to feel scared or inadequate, but remember that you are worth loving the way you are."

The strange paradox is that the behaviors we use to obscure ourselves from others, as well as from ourselves, are much less palatable than what we are attempting to hide. The problem is, few of us realize our true worth. We have been influenced since early childhood to feel fearful of not being sufficient, to feel shame for our frailties, and to feel a desperate need to be loved. These are not feelings to be ashamed of. They are human characteristics to be valued and cherished. Any good chef will tell you that the better the quality of the product you start with, the less you have to do to improve it or enhance it. The real secret to good cooking is not to alter the way something tastes but to bring out the food's natural essence.

Why should it be any different for people? Perhaps each of us has to discover the true essence of ourselves. Rather than hide from what we believe we may be or disguise what we fear ourselves to be, we need to open ourselves up sufficiently to realize the basic worth of who we are.

Step one of the two-step process involves seeing ourselves emotionally naked, and accepting the person we see. Emotional nakedness comes when we strip away the Ph.D. the master's degree, the job title, community status, the money we make, and all the other things we use to shore up our egos, and simply acknowledge that underneath it all lies a fundamentally adequate person who can make a difference in the lives of others.

Step two involves forgiving ourselves for all the past behaviors that we regret and for which we cannot make amends. If there are bridges that can be repaired, by all means make amends. The recognition, acceptance and forgiveness of the person we discover inside ourselves is the most important path we will ever take toward being able to live with ourselves in an emotionally healthy manner. The need to pour on the sauce becomes a thing of the past.

Instead, we serve ourselves up without all the embellishments. Let's face it. A good barbecued steak doesn't need a lot of sauce.

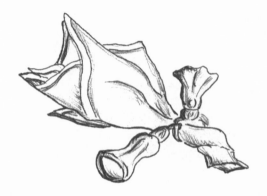

Roast Pork Loin with Cranberry Barbecue Sauce

This is so easy that you may be reluctant to try it, but when you do you'll be delighted. It feeds a crowd and I promise you, your guests will love it—especially the sauce.

1 pork loin (ask the butcher to crack the ribs and backbone
    so it will be easier to slice)
2 tablespoons olive oil
1 tablespoon garlic salt
1 tablespoon Lawry's seasoned salt
1-1/2 cups white vinegar
1 heaping tablespoon crushed red pepper flakes

Sauce
1 16-oz bottle of KC Barbecue sauce
1 can whole cranberry sauce
1/4 cup Italian dressing

Depending on how many people you're expecting, you can purchase half a loin or the center cut. I prefer using the loin with the bones because the bones help to retain moisture in the meat. Heat your grill on high heat if its gas, or wait until the coals are white-hot if using charcoal. Sear the roast on all sides and remove from the grill. Rub the meat with the olive oil and cover with garlic and seasoned salt. At this point you can return it directly to the grill or place the roast fat side up in a foil roasting pan and place it on the grill. Cover the grill and baste meat occasionally with a mixture of vinegar and red pepper flakes. Don't worry that the meat will become too hot or spicy. It doesn't. Cook meat until an instant read meat thermometer reaches an internal reading of 120°. Meanwhile, mix the sauce ingredients in a saucepan on the stovetop and heat thoroughly. You can then begin basting the roast with the cranberry sauce mixture. When the internal temperature reaches 155° to 160°, remove meat from grill and cover for 10 minutes before slicing. It is now that you will reap a second benefit of buying the loin roast. First slice along the bones lengthwise and under the bottom of the roast to remove the whole tenderloin. Then cut the rib bones apart where the butcher cracked them and you will have spareribs as well as two-inch slices of boneless pork. Serve with sauce on the side. Serves 12.

Chapter 11

Roast Duck

❋ ❋ ❋ ❋ ❋ ❋ ❋ ❋ ❋ ❋ ❋ ❋ ❋ ❋ ❋

A Chinese proverb says that a starving peasant must stand for a very long time on a high hill with his mouth open before a roast duck will fall into it. I love roast duck and if I thought it would work, I would climb that hill, stand beside the peasant and open my mouth. Of course, a roast duck is never going to fall into that starving peasant's mouth.

We shake our head at the poor peasant, but we can look around us in the world today and see an awful lot of people waiting for something to come their way without ever expending any effort or energy of their own. The risk nothing, they gain nothing. They just hope or wish.

We needn't look far to find these people. Lonely people who want to meet someone but are too frightened of rejection. Women especially, but men as well, who feel trapped in their marriages or relationships, stay and bitterly complain about their spouse or partner. Men who criticize but always search out needy, dependent women to be involved with. Women who repetitively find men they can't love because they abuse them or cheat on them.

As you might imagine, in my clinical practice I see a lot of people who wring their hands, spout platitudes and wait for someone or something to come along and deliver them from their inertia.

Larry was a 400-pound man in his late thirties who, despite his college degree, couldn't find a job. He told me he didn't have the right clothes to wear to an initial interview. His car was so desperately in need of repair that he doubted he could trust it to get him anywhere. "Besides," he said, "who would hire me in my obese state?"

I listened and I understood. Why should he set himself up for failure? Nevertheless, who could fail to observe that the 400 pounds he was carrying did not get there by accident. Even though he stood 6'2", isn't his weight evidence enough of some kind of emotional dysfunction? It would seem that he had built a 400-pound wall of fat to separate himself and estrange himself from others in his world. His girth also provided a wonderful excuse for not being able to cope with what he perceived to be an emotionally threatening, demanding, and critical world.

Jenny was forty-five years old when her husband ran off with his secretary. He left her with the kids, her emotional problems, and the family's financial difficulties. She tells anyone who will listen about the enormous burden she is carrying. Nobody, other than her family, cares about her, she's convinced, because if they did, they would have absolutely nothing to do with her husband. Ask her about dating and she goes to town: "Men don't want a woman in her forties" she responds. "They want to trade their forty-year-old in on two twenties. Besides, how could anyone expect me to trust any man again?"

For a moment, her argument sounds almost reasonable. It's easy to see that she's been hurt and is very afraid of being rejected again. But when you listen between the lines, you begin to hear clues that her willingness to trust or get emotionally close to anyone was suspect long before her marriage or her husband's involvement with another woman. Jenny learned early in life that giving gifts and performing other tangible actions were evidence that you loved someone. She thought all she had to do was stay busy, provide a clean home, cook and care for the kids, and her husband and children should know that she loved them.

In one way or another she rebuffed her husband on the numerous occasions when he asked her to run away with him for a day to walk on the beach; to sit with him for thirty minutes and forget about the house, the children and the homework; or just to have a glass of wine, listen to classical music and enjoy their relationship. These behaviors were foreign to her. She had to be doing something, washing dishes, cleaning the kitchen, putting the kids to bed, ironing, anything that would prove that she was productive and therefore worthy of being loved. I know she loved her husband, but in a way radically different from what he was looking for. Her way wasn't necessarily wrong, but she needed to look inside herself and ask what she could do differently when it was obvious that what she was doing wasn't working. Unfortunately, like many of us, she was too frightened and therefore too defensive of her old behaviors and beliefs.

I'm not condoning her husband's actions either. He could have taken responsibility for adapting his behavior to better suit what she needed as well, instead of escaping into another relationship, where he is likely to repeat his own same behavior.

Amy, an extremely attractive and bright MBA, was still single at thirty-eight, feeling empty, unable to sleep well at night and wondering, "What is it all for?" When she came to see me, there was little doubt that she was depressed. She regretted her career choice and her single life but didn't know what she could do to change things. Without her profession to hide behind, she became alarmingly aware of her loneliness. When I asked about any previous long-term relationships, she listed four or five. One was with a man who was twenty years older and lived halfway across the country. A second man was "getting a divorce" for more than two years, until Amy finally walked away. She had two or three other extended affairs with married men who were in no way considering leaving their wives. It didn't take a nuclear physicist to do the calculations. None of these men were available and, emotionally speaking, neither was Amy. Rather than face her fear, she preferred to continue playing the victim.

There was no difference between any one of the previous individuals and a young man I counseled for a year and a half. He spent the first six months of his weekly sessions (paid for by his parents) consumed with what he considered to be his major problem: He was an inch too short to be accepted into the Houston Police Academy. No alternative suggestions or solutions would satisfy him; nothing short of entering the academy was acceptable. He came to therapy, rehashed his problem, complained about his genes and voiced his anger and indignation about the rules set up by the Houston Police Department. For all intents and purposes, he was standing on a hilltop with his mouth wide open, waiting for a roast duck to fall, and blaming everyone else when the duck didn't materialize.

In every example I've presented, several common denominators prevail. Not one of the individuals above truly pursued what they claimed they wanted. They never really took a risk. They burned a lot of oxygen expressing their hopes and their wishes, but they *acted* on the basis of their fears. Each one expected good fortune or luck to carry them through. The young man who wanted to become a police officer expressed it directly, when he said, "You can't argue with what Vince Lombardi once said, 'It is better to be lucky than good.'" However, he forgot to mention that Lombardi went on to say, "But it's a strange thing; the harder my players work, the more effort they put out, the luckier they get." I suspect that principle would apply to all of us. The biggest obstacle to putting out an honest effort and making a genuine commitment is our own unconscious fear of failure, and our sense of insufficiency and inadequacy.

To get whatever we want in life requires that we win the war between ourselves and our fears. The first step in winning the war is to recognize that something is wrong, that our actions in the past have not worked, and that we must change our behavior. Next, we must learn to approach life on the basis of our desires. Third, we need to acknowledge the contradiction between our thoughts, our words, and our behavior. Fourth, it is essential that we clearly determine what our goals are and realize that neither rigid, unbending behavior nor helter-skelter, panic-driven actions will lead us to what we want. Fifth, we must learn to ask ourselves, "Is what I am doing now consistent with what I truly want? Will it make me happy when I look back twenty-four hours from now, and will I be proud of the way I behaved?" If the answer is "no," we must see that our behavior is unacceptable to us.

On the positive side, however, each of us is capable of setting goals and reaching them if we can behave in accordance with one cardinal rule: Don't Be Afraid To Fail.

Don't let your fears govern your actions and never be reluctant to try. Failure is a natural part of learning.

I once heard a speaker say, "Anything worth doing is worth failing at." Think about it. How many things have we accomplished in life that required repeated failing first? We learned to walk, but only after falling countless times. We learned to speak, but first we spent months pronouncing the words wrong. Why, as we grow older, do we exert so much energy and effort to avoid failure? Perhaps we never fully learned that failure is an essential part of the learning process. Failure is proof of our progress toward reaching the goals we claim we desire. There are no guarantees in life that following these rules will result in success, but standing on a hilltop will only lead to cooking your own goose.

Roast Duck

There are many different ways to roast a duck. This is one of my favorites. It is in part borrowed from a Chinese technique and seasoned with a peppercorn mustard crust and cider gravy. The duck is briefly placed in boiling water and then thoroughly dried with a hair dryer. The boiling water opens the skin's pores and the dryer ensures that they stay open. Later, as the duck roasts, the fat melts and runs through the open pores allowing the skin to become crisp. The gravy is a mixture of the bird's cooking juices flavored with mustard, peppercorn, apple cider and thyme.

1/4 cup plus 1 tablespoon unsalted butter
4 1/4 to 5 lb. duck
2 tablespoons flour
2 tablespoons Dijon mustard
1 tablespoon dry mustard
1 tablespoon cracked black peppercorns
1 tablespoon whole mustard seeds
2 teaspoons golden brown sugar
2 teaspoons dried thyme

Gravy
1 cup apple cider
3 tablespoons apple jack brandy
2 tablespoons flour
3/4 cup chicken broth (homemade or canned)
1 tablespoon cider vinegar
1 teaspoon Dijon mustard
salt and pepper
1/4 cup reserved duck drippings

For herb paste combine 1/4 cup butter with flour, Dijon and dry mustards, peppercorns, mustard seeds, sugar and thyme in a bowl. Reserve. Preheat the oven to 450° and position rack in lowest third of the oven. Boil water in a pot sufficiently large enough to hold the entire duck. Remove the gizzard and the gobs of fat on either side of the duck cavity. When the water comes to a boil, add the duck and return the water to a boil. After 6 minutes remove duck and pat dry with paper towels. Direct hot air from the hair dryer over the skin of the duck for 6 to 8 minutes. Melt remaining butter and rub over the entire duck. Place the duck on a roasting rack, breast side up, and cook for 30 minutes.

Spread herb paste over duck and inside cavity. Turn the oven down to 375° and cook the duck for at least 1 hour more until the skin is crisp. Remove the duck from the oven and place in a deep dish temporarily. Collect the liquid inside duck and 1/3 cup fat from the roasting pan. Place in a saucepan along with flour and stir over medium high heat until golden brown, about 2 minutes. Whisk in cider mixture and stock. Simmer until thickened, stirring occasionally, about 2 minutes. Remove from heat. Mix in cider vinegar and mustard, season with salt and pepper. Detach wings and drumsticks, and cut breast in half. Serve on a platter along with gravy in a serving boat. Serves 4.

Chapter 12

Food Talks

❋ ❋ ❋ ❋ ❋ ❋ ❋ ❋ ❋ ❋ ❋ ❋ ❋ ❋

People use food to communicate. How many hours did our mothers and grandmothers spend in the kitchen as an expression of their love? It didn't matter what language they used —"Sit down and eat," "Mangia," "Cometelo"— all say the same thing, "I love you. I want to fill your stomach and warm your heart. Now eat and show me how much you value my love."

Food can also be used as a form of punishment or a means of expressing discontent. How many times have you heard—or said—"If you don't finish everything on your plate, you don't get any dessert," or "If you don't do what I say, you can go to bed without supper." Or maybe you've heard a woman say, "After the kids leave, I'm not cooking anymore."

For some people, cooking is a way to express themselves creatively or to share warm and caring feelings. For others, preparing food is only a responsibility or a burden. In either case, it says something about the individuals involved. The same can be said for the way we deal with food. Some people eat only because they must to survive. Others, like me, read cookbooks instead of novels. There are those who order from a menu based on which item is the lowest price, and those whose selection depends on who is paying the bill. These differences are meaningful. So much of who and what we are is expressed and shown through the foods we eat, the way we eat it, the way we prepare it, and the manner in which we serve it.

Unlike the language of food, the language of people can be terribly vague, confusing, and contradictory. "No" can mean "yes," and "yes" can mean "no," and "maybe" leaves everything up in the air.

"Go away, get out of here, leave me alone" can frequently mean *I need you. Prove to me you care by not listening to my words.*

"You're only here for my money, you don't love me" can mean *Please deny it and say you really do care.*

"I'm tired, why don't you just call up some of your buddies and go out with them," seemed, to one of my patients, like a very clear-cut statement saying, *Go do your own thing this evening.* However, the next morning he heard, "I can't believe you just left me and went out for dinner with your friends. You knew I hadn't eaten. A lot you care about me."

"Do you want me to cook something?" can mean *If you really loved me, you would take me out tonight.*

"No thank you, I'm really not hungry" can mean *Please ask me again so I can accept without feeling like I'm mooching.*

"If that's what you want to do, go ahead, go!" can mean *I am losing the emotional tug-of-war, so go ahead, go on your date, or go out with the guys, but you will regret it when you come home and find your poor mother sick or dead.*

The words we use can be truly misleading. Our tongues can be a weapon that slice right through someone. It can insidiously control through guilt; it can destroy someone emotionally with criticism or put-downs; or it can hurt desperately when it implies rejection, lack of care, or a final good-bye.

Five relatively simple rules can significantly help us communicate more effectively with one another. Of course, these rules are easier to understand than to actualize. Nevertheless, I know that you can do it if you give them serious thought and devote sufficient time and conscious effort to make them work for you.

1. There is a difference between talking to someone and communicating with them. If all you want to do is talk, simply open your mouth and let the air come out—even if it's hot air. If you want to communicate, you have an added responsibility. You must expend sufficient effort to help the other person hear and understand what you have to say. Talking louder, or screaming at someone who doesn't speak your language does not help them understand. The same goes for your friends, family and spouse. If you want to be heard, you must deliver your message as many ways as it takes until the other person truly comprehends your message. They may not necessarily agree, but if they understand what you intended to communicate, then you have communicated effectively. The goal of successful communication is to reach another human being.

2. Eliminate the word "you" from your vocabulary if you truly want to reach someone. When *you* say "you" to someone, eventually you will elicit their ire. It's inevitable.

Some examples: You said a dumb thing. You don't understand. You are always late. You don't get involved with the kids. You work all the time. You are lazy and irresponsible. You are drunk. Statements such as these cannot help but raise the hair on the back of anyone's neck. They do not lay a foundation for a warm, interactive relationship. The word to use is "I," as in "I feel that I am not reaching you but I want to and I will continue to try as long as you will listen."

Years ago, I had a patient who was totally infuriated over his wife's apparent inability to understand what he thought was a simple business concept. Finally in total frustration, he yelled, "You are just too thick to understand this concept." It was then that I told him about the substitution of "I" for "you." I gave him several examples, such as, "I feel completely frustrated trying to explain this concept to you. I'm certain that is because I am unable to communicate it in a way you can understand —"

He interrupted me and said, "I understand what you are saying. Instead of saying 'you are so thick,' I should have said, 'I feel you are thick headed.'"

Obviously, *I* had not communicated in a way that he could understand. What he could have said was, "I feel so thick headed. I can't seem to explain this to you adequately. If I seem short tempered or upset, it is myself I am frustrated with, not you."

3. We must be honest in our communication. If we lie, if we cover up, if we sugar coat what we are saying, the other person will not be able to hear what is truly bothering us. Consequently, they won't be able to understand what is broken and they won't see a need to fix it. Unfortunately, honesty is the quality most often lacking in communication. In many instances we hedge because we really do not want to hurt another human being; but in the process of trying not to hurt, we frequently wind up hurting them far more and far longer. The majority of us are rarely fully honest with

one another, except when we are extremely angry. Then it is difficult to determine whether our emotions are expressions of honesty or a form of hostility. The two have little in common, except they both begin with the same letter of the alphabet. Without honesty, we never achieve healthy communication, we only create deceit.

4. Good communicators, not only know *how* to say things, but *when* to say them and how to *listen* as well. Listening requires not only hearing the words, but also comprehending the message. To listen acutely we must learn to understand the silences, to hear what is conveyed between the lines, and to be able to interpret body language and verbal intonations. Effective listening is difficult. Too often, we fail to hear what is being said, because we assume a totally defensive orientation. We emotionally prepare to attack and we only hear what we fear.

The best example I can give is that of a forty-two-year-old physician who married an extremely attractive twenty-six-year-old woman after a prolonged divorce that was both emotionally and financially expensive. The young lady he married was but bright, educated, and able to recognize her own immaturity. She was willing to work at developing better communication skills in order to improve her relationship with her new husband and her new stepchildren, who were not much younger than she was.

However, early in their marriage, after two weeks of almost constant upset and turmoil, the couple came to physical blows and threats of divorce. Her husband felt he was being bombarded from every side. No matter which way he turned somebody was after him.

His son was graduating from high school and wanted a new car. But not just any car; he wanted one that cost twice as much as his father had planned to spend. The physician's ex-wife was taking him back to court seeking additional support. His younger teenage daughter needed extensive orthodontic work, which he was willing to pay for, but she also wanted to go to Europe for the summer, which was too much to ask.

My patient's father, who was a ne'er-do-well, a borderline alcoholic, and a chronic gambler, quit his job and asked for financial support for himself and *his* new wife. In the midst of all this, the doctor's young bride spoke to him about new living room furniture that he had agreed to purchase. Her timing was terrible.

The doctor blew up. He lost emotional control and in the course of his rage, he called his wife "a money-hungry manipulative selfish witch (with a "B")," who was trying to suck him dry. "You are no different," he said, "from everybody else out there trying to get what they want from me." She launched into her own tirade and threatened to pack and leave by the end of the week. He was incredulous. He could not comprehend her reaction and felt that what he had said was far more prophetic than he had realized.

What she had done was listen to his words and personalize his accusations without ever hearing his message. Had she been in a better frame of mind herself, she might have heard that what he was really saying was, "I can't take it anymore. Everywhere I turn somebody wants something from me. No one cares for me. The handwriting on the wall is pretty plain. If I don't come through, I don't love you. Even more distressing, all of you won't love me. I just wish there was someone here to support me, to love me and to tell me that I don't have to pay for love." If she had heard those words she would have been there for him. She forgot, or never knew, that good communication requires that we listen acutely, not to the words, but to the message, which is often conveyed between the lines or disguised by anger and defensiveness.

5. It is essential to learn that we all speak different emotional languages. It is possible for two people to say the same thing, but say it so differently that neither one recognizes that they are in agreement. Let me give you an example. I came from a poor socioeconomic background. It wasn't that we didn't have food, there just wasn't always a lot of it. Thus, what you got, you ate! Nothing was wasted. There was no room for having bigger eyes than your stomach. You had to finish everything you put on your plate. Although my wife came from a similar socioeconomic background, her family had a radically different attitude toward food. Her grandmother, who raised her, was a chef in the Catskills and consequently there was always food to be found in their home. On our honeymoon, I recall sitting in a small restaurant in Key West, Florida. When Harriet's lunch arrived, she took her sandwich, cut the crusts off the four edges of her bread and left them on her plate along with some of her meal. At the same time, in accordance with everything I had learned as a child, I ate every crumb on my plate. I then proceeded to finish everything on her plate. In my own way, I was saying to her, "Look, I am finishing everything on my plate and yours. You should love me." Meanwhile, she was saying, "I am watching my weight and leaving things on my plate, so you should love me. In my mind she had no regard for the "starving children in China," a phrase I heard frequently as a youngster. At the same time, she was probably afraid that if there was anything else edible on the table, I would eat it. Our genuine messages of love were invisible to each other and thus impossible to perceive. We needed an intensive course in understanding each other.

The more I deal with people and their problems, the more I think we can learn from food and the way it talks to us. I know how much better all of our relationships would be if we could only communicate clearly and to the point. To that end, we need to listen a little better, respond a little slower, demonstrate a great deal more compassion and understanding for one another and follow my five basic rules: communicate, don't just talk; express feelings in terms of "I," not "you"; insist on honesty; discover when to listen and when to talk; and learn to decode your partner's language of love. Only then will our communication skills become as nourishing and meaningful as the food on our plate.We will learn how to say, in effect, "Eat, eat. I want to fill your stomach and warm your heart with my gifts of love."

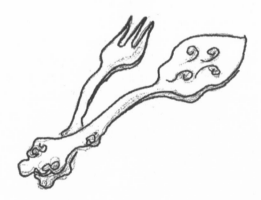

Cajun Turkey

No food speaks louder to us than Roast Turkey. It says holiday, family, and celebration all at the same time. This bird, in particular, really says a mouthful. Our Thanksgiving tradition changed after the first time I tried this recipe. Now I make two turkeys each year. One is a traditional bird with a bread stuffing. The other is the Cajun Turkey, which always disappears from the table first. It is the easiest turkey you will ever cook, but you have to follow the recipe to a T. Fortunately there are no difficult steps and, if your family and friends like spicy food, you will receive more accolades than you can imagine.

1 22 to 25 lb. self-basting turkey
1 lb. butter, margarine or butter substitute
1 large roaster pan or two flat bottomed disposable
    aluminum roasters stacked together to accommodate
    the bird's weight

Spice mixture A
1 teaspoon Lawry's garlic powder
1 teaspoon Lawry's seasoned salt
1/4 teaspoon celery seeds

Spice mixture B
1/2 cup seasoned salt
1/3 cup seasoned pepper
1 tablespoon cayenne pepper
1/2 teaspoon poultry seasoning
1/2 teaspoons celery seeds
1 tablespoon garlic powder

Rinse and dry bird inside and out. Season the cavity with spice mixture "A." Line the sink with paper towels. Put the turkey in the sink, bottom-side up, and coat with 2 sticks margarine. Use a pastry brush in order to cover all the joints and every inch of the turkey. Sprinkle 1/4 of spice mixture "B" over the margarine-coated turkey. Put the turkey, bottom side down, into the pan. Repeat process on top and sides. Use all of spice mixture "B," skin should not be visible. Lastly, add 1 stick margarine in the pan and bake the turkey at 225° for 10 to 12 hours with no cover or rack in the roaster. Basting is not needed, but when I'm not lazy I baste the top of the turkey with the remaining margarine after a several hours of baking. You can bake the turkey the night before and it will be ready the following morning. NOTE: Do not release drumsticks from skin holding them together. Save the juice to spoon over slices when serving. If making a smaller turkey, 18 to 20 lbs, adjust cooking time to approximately 8 to 9 hours.

Chapter 13

Gathering the Honey

✳ ✳ ✳ ✳ ✳ ✳ ✳ ✳ ✳ ✳ ✳ ✳ ✳ ✳ ✳

One of my favorite birds to cook is quail. I usually marinate the little critters in a combination of teriyaki, soy and Worcestershire sauce with a little brown sugar. The secret, however, is that after they have browned pretty well on the grill, I baste them with pure honey, which caramelizes and coats them beautifully. I get my honey the easy way, off the supermarket shelf. But honey doesn't naturally come in a glass or plastic container. The bee keeper has to manually collect this wonderful nectar from his beehives. The price he pays is the risk of being stung. To defend himself he typically dresses in protective clothing, including a hat with netting that either drops over his shoulders or closes around his neck in order to prevent any bees from stinging his face. Nevertheless, despite the beekeeper's best efforts, some very persistent bees occasionally find their way under his clothes. Ouch!

Other collecting techniques involve laying down a cloud of smoke to dull the activities of the bees so that the keeper can obtain the honey with less risk of being hurt.

Another, more radical, approach would be to kill the bees—just destroy the whole hive. The destruction method eliminates any possibility of injury and makes every last lick of honey available. Of course, this method only works once, and would be akin to killing the goose that lays the golden eggs.

The most successful beekeepers overcome their fear of being stung (or they somehow develop an immunity to bee stings). As a result, they are able to approach the hives gently and collect the honey, while only mildly disturbing the bees.

Throughout my years as a therapist, I have seen countless patients utilizing all of the approaches described above. I have watched couples who are dating, husbands and wives, parents and children, experience pain and inflict pain while they all searched for the same thing: the "honey" of emotional nourishment. Their success, the amount of pain they experience, and the satisfaction they derive from obtaining this honey, which we call love, depends on the method of collection they choose.

Some of us are so afraid of being stung that we never even risk collecting the love we want. We never approach the hive. Why open up and give someone the chance to hurt you or reject you? More often than not, we are blind to our avoidance behavior. Running and hiding is a totally unconscious process. In therapy, I have heard many attractive, intelligent, professional women lament for the entire hour how lonely and depressed they are. Their phone rarely rings, the only men they meet are losers, and they have a gaggle of girlfriends who will verify how terrible single life is.

How do people find, enjoy, and commit to one another? What makes the difference? Do some people have a "Vacancy" sign hanging around their necks, while others have a sign saying "Full—No Rooms Available"? I believe that's true (obviously speaking figuratively). I further believe that birds of a feather flock together, so it's no surprise when I hear that my patients have friends whose lives are similar to theirs.

Collecting the honey of love involves taking chances and exposing yourself emotionally to an available partner. It means not entering into affairs with married individuals or chasing after someone whose track record includes numerous involvements, few commitments and a trail of broken hearts. After all, why would you think it would be any different with you?

Unlike real honey, you cannot get love by buying it, though many of us try. Instead of being honest, we give in to those we love. We capitulate, acquiesce, and prostitute our values. Some of us even accept emotional or physical abuse. The end result is always the same. We wind up resenting the people we love and blaming them for mistreating us, when our real anger is toward ourselves because of our own poor sense of worth and our inability to stand up.

Others of us go through life wearing all kinds of protective behaviors, which are designed to minimize our hurt or vulnerability but in the end serve only to drive others away rather than attract them. These behaviors range from one extreme to the other. Someone who plays the role of the weak, self-righteous victim can hardly hold a candle to a partner who is capable of saying, "I truly don't need you. I am capable of making it on my own, but I want you because I love you. I see your weaknesses but I know your strengths. I love the soft, intuitive person I see inside you and I want to share my life with you."

The excessively tough, independent and self-sufficient individual is no better off. His attitude implies that
he doesn't need anyone. It says to a partner that she is
neither wanted nor valued. It is easy to understand how
vulnerable that partner would be to someone who says,
"You are so important to me. You add meaning to my life
and I feel so much more a person because you are there
for me."

In either instance, settling for the non-emotional,
independent and insulated individual or the helpless,
dependent martyr is like using a sugar substitute. Neither
relationship is conducive to creating an environment in
which honest love can grow. But many of us avoid honest
love, albeit unconsciously. Some of us prefer someone who
is distant, insulated or estranged, because they demand little
from us emotionally. Others seem to prefer a pseudo-
involvement with a dependent, needy individual who will
look up to them and never consider leaving.

The smoke-screen approach is radically different.
What you see is not what you get. These individuals make
far better dates than spouses. Before there is a commitment,
they are able to produce a smoke screen of loving
sweetness. However, it rapidly disappears after the rice is
thrown or when the children begin to arrive. By that time,
you realize that you have been hoodwinked. There is no real
"honey." You wind up feeling betrayed and angry. And
chances are, you've felt this way before, because until we
we learn to control our lives with our heads instead of our
hearts, we will unconsciously choose the same type of
person over and over again. Following our heads instead of
our hearts only comes with emotional health. When our
hearts are emotionally accustomed to pick someone who
will disappoint us, that's who we'll choose every time. Then

we either leave the relationship or stay, feeling trapped, emotionally cheated, and stung.

There is nothing positive that can be said about the destruction method—killing a relationship you value because of your own fear of rejection or hurt. Without a doubt, destroying a relationship is excessive behavior, overkill, like shooting a canary with a cannon; but I see it every day. I watch people destroy relationships when they come to realize their need for them. Think how many "perfect" marriages you have seen end in divorce just about the time when everything looks ideal. The couple is finally out of debt. The kids are out of college. The new house is finally finished. The decorator just delivered the last piece of furniture, and suddenly the couple is telling it to the judge. Why? They claim they have nothing left in common. Perhaps a more accurate statement would be that they have nothing left to preoccupy or distract themselves. They finally have the opportunity to be close to one another, to love each other without interruption, and then they blow it all up. They are unwilling to risk honest hurt or abandonment and are reluctant to face the reality that they never learned how to love intimately. They knew how to live together, eat together, and sleep together. But loving together was never in their repertoire. Oh, they call it love and often in therapy they will say that their "love died." I frequently ask, "How? Pneumonia? Cancer? Upper respiratory disease? Or neglect?" In any case, they break up a marriage that might have provided the emotional nourishment they both desired if only they knew or cared to learn how to collect it and taste it. Instead, they blame their partner for their problems, become supersensitive to minor hurts and look for someone or something else to preoccupy themselves.

There is another way to deal with our fear of emotional hurt. I have heard that people with severe allergies can sometimes build immunities to local flowers, weeds, and pollen by consuming honey made by bees from their local community. It seems there may be an analogy here. What if we search for sweetness and goodness in our present partners in our present marriages before we leave or "destroy" them? Is it possible that we might develop feelings so positive that the occasional hurts and stings that lovers inflict on one another would be of little consequence? Of course, this would require that we deal with our partners gently and kindly. The latter is only possible when we learn to behave out of our desires instead of our fears. I do not want to say that this will always work. Occasionally we come across a hive of killer bees, but that is the exception, not the rule. The rule is that when you want honey, you must gently approach the hive. In other words, you give love to get it. When you get it, you have to return it, because that's what keeps the love alive. And if occasionally you get stung, look beyond it and enjoy the honey. It's worth it.

Honey Quail

This dish can be part of an antipasto or served as a main course. Quail are now raised domestically and are readily available in specialty food stores or supermarkets, usually in the frozen foods section. Simply defrost them, cut them in half with scissors and marinate them.

8 quail (16 halves)
honey
1 teaspoon Dijon mustard or apricot jelly
seasoned salt and pepper to taste

Marinade
1 cup water
2 chicken bouillon cubes
1 cup soy sauce
1/2 cup Worcestershire sauce
1 cup honey

Place the quail in a glass baking pan. In a saucepan, bring the marinade mixture to a boil and simmer briefly. Pour the marinade over the quail and sprinkle with seasoned salt and pepper. Cover and refrigerate for several hours, or better yet, overnight.

When ready to cook, remove the quail from the marinade and place them on a hot grill, bone side down. After they are browned, turn them over and baste the cooked side with a mixture made up primarily of honey with a small amount of the marinade and, depending on how you feel, add a teaspoon of apricot jelly. After the skin side has browned, turn them for the second time, browning the basted side until the skin begins to darken. Meanwhile I baste the skin side with the honey-marinade, and apricot mixture and turn them over for one more time. It sounds more complicated than it is, and the results are well worth it. If you choose not to barbecue, you can achieve similar results under the broiler. Serves 8 as an appetizer or 4 as a main course.

Chapter 14

There's More Than One Way to Cook a Chicken

❊ ❊ ❊ ❊ ❊ ❊ ❊ ❊ ❊ ❊ ❊ ❊ ❊ ❊

I have loved to cook ever since I was a child. When I was young, cooking served many purposes, both good and bad. It was a way of proving that I was a good kid, helpful and involved. It allowed me to garner some accolades for my achievements and to demonstrate my worth—although not all of my products were received with great joy or overwhelming compliments. Cooking helped me to try to satisfy an inner feeling of emptiness, which I filled primarily with food. As I mentioned before, it was no surprise that I was a fat little guy. But my real involvement with cooking started on my twenty-fifth wedding anniversary. Harriet and I gave each other the same present, a two-week vacation in Italy, including eight days at a cooking school in Bologna, run by Marcella Hazan and her husband, Victor. Among the many places we have traveled and the things we have done, that course still holds a very special place in our hearts. It was there that we learned a true love for cooking.

We arrived in Bologna by train. From the station, we took a cab to the hotel where Marcella conducted her classes and where we would stay. We unpacked and anxiously waited to meet our mentor and the other students. The group consisted of eighteen individuals, soon to be sixteen, from assorted backgrounds, professions, and ages. All shared one common interest, a love for food and its preparation. During our introductory meeting with Marcella, one of the group members asked, "Will you be giving us a workbook or menus to follow?" Her answer was, "No, if you came here to get recipes, then you have wasted an awful lot of money. You could have bought all of my cookbooks and found the recipes for many more dishes than you will learn to prepare here. This week I hope to take you beyond the recipes and provide you with an opportunity to immerse yourself in a total food experience. I want you to be able to appreciate the many different ways that the same food can be prepared and to discover the joy in its preparation. I want you to learn not to be afraid to get your hands wet, dirty, or sticky; and most of all, I want you to be able to overcome any fears you have of the kitchen, of preparing food, and of entertaining."

Her words were no doubt disappointing to some in the group, because many human beings feel far more secure with something tangible to hold on to. Specific guidelines and instructions provide emotional security, which helps to quell their fear of making a mistake or failing. Consequently, it was no surprise to me when a couple from Seattle, Washington, suddenly began to complain about their hotel accommodations and the poor quality of what I thought was an unbelievably delicious welcoming banquet at a local Michelin three-star restaurant. Several hours later, they left with their bags packed. I suspect that the perceived lack of structure created more anxiety for them than they could tolerate. From their viewpoint, Marcella's approach probably looked like a lack of preparation or poor planning—a very believable explanation for their friends and family when they arrived home. By rationalizing that their experience was Marcella's fault, they could justify their own actions and curtail the need for deeper introspective examination.

For me, Marcella's words were pure joy, because the things she said are exactly what I try to convey to every one of my therapy patients. I want to assist them in discovering the joy of living. I want to help them eliminate their fear of expressing themselves, of dealing with others, and of taking risks in life. And more than anything else, I hope they will hear that there is more than one way to live life and there is no magic recipe for dealing with people.

I once had a patient who told me a story about his youth. When Paul was fourteen, in the latter stages of puberty, his hormones were raging but he had no clue about the opposite sex. In a desperate search for answers, he sought the advice of a fifteen-year-old buddy who he thought was extremely mature and knowledgeable about women. With an air of great authority, his friend assured him that there was a secret to gaining the favor of any woman in the world. The trick was blowing in her ear, which was unequivocally guaranteed to bring any woman to a point of wild and uncontrollable sexual craving. Fortified with this information, Paul built up his courage and began his quest. From then on, he blew in the ear of every woman he got close to. The result was that most of them wondered whether he had an asthmatic problem or something else seriously wrong with him. In no case, however, did his little trick achieve the desired results. You see, there truly is no single, magic recipe for giving or receiving love.

I suspect that you have heard the story about the woman cooking her Easter ham who called up her middle sister to ask her why, when they were growing up, their mother always cut the ham in half before she baked it. Her middle sister had no idea and suggested to call their older sister for the answer. The eldest sister was equally unaware and suggested they call Mom and ask her. With great care, so as not to seem critical, they said to her, "Mother, all of our adult lives, each of us has followed your recipe whenever we bake a ham. The first thing we do is cut it in half and we all wonder why we do that." Without a second's hesitation, their mother responded, "I really don't know why the three of you do it, but the reason I did was because I didn't have a pan large enough to hold the whole ham." Isn't that just like life? We learn how to love each other and relate to others without any real rhyme or reason. As adults, we end up unconsciously emulating the role models we had in our youth.

Here's a specific example from therapy, which may help you to clearly see this process in action. Claude and Marie have been married for sixteen years. Each was married before. Claude's first marriage ended on an extremely bad note when he left his wife—who was cold, unresponsive, sad and depressed—for Marie, who was vivacious, responsive, sensual and sexual. Marie was everything that Claude wished his first wife could have been. Their courtship was a whirlwind of excitement, love, and lust. Marie's first marriage was to a highly critical, fault-finding, aggressively angry man who caused her to feel unloved and unworthy.

Sixteen years later, this second marriage could well be described in the same terms as their first. You see, Claude and Marie only brought to their relationship what they had learned during childhood and practiced in their previous marriages. Neither one knew that they could not achieve the long-term happiness they were seeking by simply changing the stove they cooked on. What they needed was cooking lessons. Cooking lessons would have shown them that using the same recipes learned earlier in life would cook up the same results every time. Chances are, the recipe had only marginally worked for their parents, and Claude and Marie had each proven in their first marriages that the recipe didn't work for them all.

Had they learned to cook, to continue with our metaphor, they would have known that they had the option to alter the ingredients and instructions in the original recipe. In life, as in the kitchen, you must not be governed by a fear of failing. In the kitchen, if you find yourself short on an ingredient, you can make a substitution. For example, one cup of apple juice for a 1/2 cup of oil tastes great and reduces the amount of fat. Two egg whites for one whole egg is any easy way to reduce cholesterol. Try two cups of oats ground in a blender as a substitute for one cup of white flour. The oats add flavor, texture and fiber

In a healthy marriage, each spouse must recognize that neither one is perfect. They both have their shortcomings and they're usually not the same ones. Often, what is perceived as a shortcoming is merely a difference in approach. Thus, a husband can sometimes balance his wife's sensitivity and insight with his practicality and ability to analyze. Meanwhile, her flair for creativity and adventure offsets his methodical discipline. The combination is a wonderful product, where each partner contributes equally, though differently, and both feel valuable and worthwhile.

Claude and Marie were too fearful to risk modifying the recipe to suit their individual tastes. They didn't know the difference between a cook and a chef. A cook has learned the proper techniques and can follow a recipe. A chef is a cook who is courageous enough to add her own taste and ideas to a recipe. A chef will try browning a chicken for about thirty or forty minutes at 400 degrees before adding it to soup in order to intensify the flavor. A chef will discover that substituting potato cooking water for other liquid is a secret ingredient for making a chocolate cake. Chefs invest a bit of themselves in their recipes, no matter what the *Ladies Home Journal* suggests or the woman down the street does. Good cooking is no different than any good relationship. You must be prepared to invest yourself in your partner.

Claude and Marie never thought to ask each other, or their original spouses, what they would find palatable or pleasing. Consequently, twice they took what could have been good relationships and destroyed them. Today, they are both taking lessons to learn how not to make the same mistake again.

The problem I see, over and over again, is that most patients want a recipe. They want a specific list of instructions telling them exactly what to do in their relationships. Why? Because it is a way of abdicating responsibility. It eliminates risk and enables us to blame someone else for our failures. It is emotionally safe and emotionally costly at the same time, because it prevents us from behaving according to who we are. Even worse, following a step-by-step procedure does not permit us to discover that we are unique, distinctive, and worthy of love.

I tell every patient I see, "Don't give away your identity. Don't become another product of a cookie cutter world." There are far too many people walking through life that way. Instead, discover yourself, show yourself, give of yourself and enjoy yourself. These are the essential ingredients for successfully creating your own recipe for a lifelong, loving relationship.

Roast Chicken with Lemons

In tribute to Marcella Hazan, I'm including this recipe, which illustrates her philosophy that good cooking needn't be complicated or complex. Simply start with top quality products, combine them and the result is a marriage that brings out the best in each ingredient. This is similar to what you wish people would do in their relationships.

Because there are truly more ways than one to cook a chicken, I have modified Marcella's "Chicken With Two Lemons" recipe by adding lemon pepper, paprika, and Lawry's seasoned salt, and cooking it at a bit higher temperature to obtain a crispier skin. The basic idea, however, belongs to her.

1 3 to 4 lb chicken
2 lemons to fit inside the chicken
Lawry's seasoned salt
Lemon pepper to taste
Paprika to taste

Preheat the oven to 425°. Wash the chicken in cold water. Remove extra fat and pat dry inside and out. Sprinkle seasoned salt and lemon pepper inside chicken. Wash lemons, place in microwave on medium setting (5) for one minute. Puncture each lemon about 15 times with a toothpick and place inside the chicken. Sew the skin around body cavity with a trussing needle and thread. Tie legs of chicken loosely with trussing thread, leaving them in a normal position. Rub the outside surface of the chicken with butter. Sprinkle outside of chicken liberally with lemon pepper, seasoned salt, and paprika. Place in a preheated shallow roasting pan in the middle of the oven. Do not cover or baste the chicken.

Roast for 1 hour, turn heat down to 375° and bake an additional 20 minutes or until thigh registers 165° to 170° on an instant temperature thermometer. The chicken presents well whole and the juices that run out as you cut the chicken up are wonderful. Serves 4.

Chapter 15

Truth in Labeling

✳ ✳ ✳ ✳ ✳ ✳ ✳ ✳ ✳ ✳ ✳ ✳ ✳ ✳ ✳

People don't shop the way they used to. Years ago, they walked into a grocery store, grab a cart and they were off to the races. They cruised the aisles, tossing in an ample supply of cookies, devil's-food cake, crackers, potato chips, pastries, and an assortment of canned creamed soups. They raided the dairy case to load up on whole milk, cottage cheese, sour cream and all kinds of cheese, the creamier the better. Topping off the cart would be an assortment of soda pop, plenty of bread, and a variety of lunch meats.

The grocery list is radically different today. Walk up and down the aisles in a supermarket and you will notice people carefully scrutinizing the labels on cans, boxes of cereal and cartons of milk. You will hear them talking about not eating carrots because they have too much natural sugar, and watching out for hidden additives and the mislabeling of so-called low-fat products.

Most of us have learned how to decipher label language. We know that "lower fat" means "less fat than the regular high-fat product." And "no sugar added" doesn't mean no sugar. We recognize the negative effects of caffeine, the virtues of fiber, and the dangerous elements of different kinds of fat. We are well versed in what we need on a daily basis to sustain life, to enhance life, and to increase life expectancy. In the vitamin section, we openly share opinions about which pill will decrease cholesterol, safeguard us from cancer or cause our hair to grow. I recently overheard a saleswoman say, "This will absolutely stimulate the growth of your hair but it will also decrease your sex drive. The hard part," she continued, "is to decide which is of greater importance." She never cracked a smile.

Today's shoppers seem to expend more time and energy determining which brand of food to purchase than they do in choosing a lifetime partner.

It is a terrible commentary to make, but it appears to me, despite everything we say to the contrary, that we direct more thought to choosing between Frosted Flakes and Raisin Bran than we do to selecting a spouse. When we finally do choose a partner, some of us believe we used our heads. Some of us claim we followed our hearts. For me, neither is true. I doubt that many of us ever consider the contents. Instead, we respond to the outside package and the flood of advertising poured out by the manufacturer. We choose our partners blindly, unconsciously, and without any intellectual awareness. We sound wise but act without reason.

No wonder so many of our marriages after a short time wind up like a diabetic in an insulin coma. Early in our marriages, we absorb all the sugar and sweets that are available and then we find ourselves unable to utilize the excess insulin we have manufactured. At times like these, a diabetic must quickly ingest additional sugar, like orange juice or a candy bar, to burn off the insulin. A love-starved partner, on the other hand, frequently searches for sugar somewhere else.

The problem is threefold. We never recognize or fully accept our own needs; we never read the other person's label (or they don't have one); or our label or our partner's label is a counterfeit. Like a manufacturer who is afraid that people would not buy his product if they knew how much fat it contained, very often we are reluctant to present ourselves as we truly are. We are too frightened to take the chance of discovering whether others will love us for ourselves. Consequently, we create dishonest labels that are products of wishful thinking or that conform to what we feel is appropriate or acceptable.

Some of us go through life with no label at all. After all, if we see in ourselves the very things we fear and can't accept, how can we possibly afford to show that self to anyone? We print a deceptive label because we are certain that no one would buy the truth.

Then there are the chameleons, who go through life with a pocket full of labels. They have one for every occasion and appear willing to give up their identities to please or appease others. Whatever the situation demands they pull out the proper tag. If you want sugar, we'll be sweet. If you want fiber, we have bulk. If you want all-business, we'll be more professional. If it's fun and games, we can be carefree. This may sound manipulative and even dishonest, but more than anything it's disheartening.

Even worse, the result is devastating. Almost sixty percent of all marriages end in divorce, because no one can keep up the act forever.

Perhaps the solution is to review our own labels to see whether we are guilty of false advertising, to check if our labels accurately depict who we really are. If your labels are not honest, if your intimate relationships are in a shambles because of your duplicity, let me give you hope. There is a healthy alternative. You can begin today to write an honest label.

If you are married, you can improve the relationship you already have. If you are single, it is time to become part of the exception rather than the rule. Most singles present themselves as someone their own mothers would hardly recognize. They hide their frailties, minimize their fears and disguise their insecurities. They distort their own realities by exaggerating their backgrounds, or create false impressions of their monetary status by spending beyond their means and neglect to mention financial difficulties. They omit their previous history regarding a divorce or having children and create deceptive images. It is a snow job of the highest order that is justified by the socially accepted practice of "putting your best foot forward." Only later, sometimes not until years after the marriage ceremony, they drag in the other foot. No wonder so many individuals in committed relationships yell, "You don't love me, you don't even know me." Whose fault is that? The self-help books that recommend playing games and using strategies to find a mate, really only help us to recruit, catch, or trap a partner. Their advice has nothing to do with developing a relationship that will stand the test of time. To do that, we need to avoid playing games and follow a "truth-in-labeling" practice.

Honest labels can help us make better choices of partners. Honest labels are essential for building and sustaining existing relationships. Honest labels help us understand how external behavior reflects internal feelings.

Perhaps you've heard the story about a man riding a commuter train in the suburbs of Boston. On this particular day, he was preoccupied with a problem at work. When he got on the train, he discovered to his chagrin that the passengers included three youngsters approximately six to twelve years old. The children were loud and making a nuisance of themselves. They ran up and down the aisle, jumping on the seats and behaving in a generally unacceptable manner. The man who appeared to be accompanying them seemed oblivious to their rowdy behavior. Finally, in exasperation, the businessman spoke sharply to the father, "Your children are impolite, rude, and desperately in need of discipline." He further elaborated, that if the man was incapable of controlling them, he should move the children and himself to another car. The man looked up with an almost dazed expression and, apologetically said, "I'm truly sorry. I know you are right, but we just left the hospital where their mother died." The businessman's anger subsided immediately and in its place came compassion and care. You see, understanding serves as an effective means of improving relationships.

A patient of mine named Marty, was married to a man fifteen years her senior. Her father had abandoned her family when she was five years old, but over the next thirteen years, Marty's mother continued to portray him as a wonderful man despite the fact that he never visited, wrote, sent cards, or provided child support. Marty felt strongly that her father didn't care, and by virtue of her mother's behavior, Marty could not believe that her mother was honest or there to protect her. Consequently, Marty mistrusted her mother emotionally. At the same time, her older brother's response to the home situation was to express his pain by emotionally abusing his sister. By the time she grew up and moved out, Marty viewed herself as unloved and unlovable. After all, every significant person in her life had treated her the same way.

Marty was totally devastated when her husband announced to their attorney that because he had owned his business before he and Marty were married, he would do whatever he pleased with the company and its assets. Part of his plans included going into a partnership with a woman who would solely own the company in the event of his death. All this in spite of the fact that Marty had worked side by side with her husband for the past ten years to make their business the success it was and never once asked for, or received, a paycheck.

Out of her deep hurt over his decision, she screamed, "I should ask for a divorce. You don't care about me; you are nothing more than a selfish, chauvinistic, uncaring son of a bitch. You have used me all these years." His response was predictably defensive, critical, and angry. He served notice that he would never be controlled by anyone, let alone his wife. Furthermore, if she didn't appreciate how generous he had been all these years, then she could just pick herself up and move out. In the words of our commuter, she could move herself to another car.

During a later visit, I asked Marty whether, in spite of her hurt, she would try to explain to her husband what she felt instead of telling him what he was. We went over the words and thoughts she might use. Then, with difficulty, she went home and said, "All my life I have felt alone. I was afraid to trust anyone emotionally. I always knew that if I had to, I could make it on my own. You are the first person I truly learned to trust and depend on. With you I let my guard down. I opened my heart. But the other day, in the lawyer's office, I felt totally betrayed. I suddenly felt that my father, my mother, and brother were right. I wasn't worth loving and I had to leave or run so I wouldn't be hurt again. I still love you but I don't believe you or anyone else will love me back."

The response she elicited this time was radically different from the one she received the first time around. I cannot guarantee that it will always work that way, but I am positive that the chances of a happy ending in any relationship are vastly increased by allowing others to clearly see us and to understand where we are coming from. Marty's words were the honest label that provided that understanding.

Because of the many situations I have seen similar to Marty's, I have come to believe that people, like food products, should be required to have informational labels. We could call them people tags. These people tags would list the ingredients, and the care, preparation and precautions necessary in dealing with the contents of the person we are interested in. Much like the tags we find on mattresses and pillows, it might include the warning "Do not remove this tag under penalty of law."

My tag would read something like this: "Hi, I'm Dr. Ed, a high-maintenance person emotionally. I require more than the average attention and nurturing. When I feel rejected, unloved, insecure, or a failure, I can become loud and angry, but my bark is far worse than my bite. Actually, I have very little bite, and although I require a great deal of input, I am willing to return the love I receive two- or threefold. When I am threatened, I tend to eat more, control more, and work more. Please do not try to change me or make me into what you want me to be. It has taken a great deal of time and effort for me to learn to accept myself for who I am. If you cannot love me for who and what I am, please look for someone else who might fit you better."

To write your own label, you must be able to objectively look at yourself and be honestly introspective. Truth in labeling requires the courage not only to see yourself, but also to share what we have discovered with someone else. In essence, it requires that we first learn to accept and love ourselves with our scars, our bumps, and our warts and then be willing to risk being rejected by someone we love and whom we want to care for us. This is not an easy task. It is, nevertheless, a risk worth taking. It is the only way to ensure that the partner we eventually attract is one who not only knows us for what we are, but likes and accepts what he knows about us and is willing to commit to the real us, not the counterfeit image so many of us project. Truth in labeling improves your chances of getting what you want, and what you are willing to live with for the rest of your life.

Crispy Spicy Sautéed Red Snapper

Perhaps no other food is mislabeled more often than fish. Only a trained eye and an experienced palate can determine between similar species. And talk about counterfeit labels! The same fish goes by different names from one part of the country to another. But regardless of the correct name, fresh fillets of firm, white meat from snapper, redfish, or trout will do for this recipe. You will be amazed by the positive but almost bewildered reactions you receive from your guests when they try to guess what you used in the coating for the fish. It's pleasantly spicy and crispy, doesn't hide the taste of the fish but adds another dimension to the meal.

4 six-ounce fillets of red snapper
2 eggs beaten well
1 bag jalapeño potato chips
2 tablespoons butter
1 tablespoon olive oil
2 teaspoons lemon pepper
sea salt to taste
wedges of lemon for garnish

Heat butter and oil in a large skillet over medium high heat. Mix eggs, salt, and lemon pepper thoroughly. Crush jalapeño potato chips with a rolling pin in a cookie baking pan or in a large piece of folded foil. Dip fillets in egg mixture and then in potato chip crumbs. Cover both sides of fish. Saute in hot oil about 10 minutes per inch of thickness, do not overcook. Serves 4.

I usually accompany the fish with the following sauce, which I make ahead of time.

Sauce

2 each of red, yellow and green bell peppers, seeded and
     cut lengthwise in 3/8 inch strips
2 large onions cut in medium slices
2 or 3 Roma tomatoes chopped into cubes
3 cloves garlic minced
2 teaspoons of dried basil, oregano, and crushed red
     pepper flakes
1/4 cup olive oil

Heat olive oil in a medium-size skillet over medium
high heat. Add all of the ingredients and cook until tender
but still firm.

Chapter 16

Lessons From a Lobster

❊ ❊ ❊ ❊ ❊ ❊ ❊ ❊ ❊ ❊ ❊ ❊ ❊ ❊ ❊

What can you learn from a lobster that will help you to live your life free of feeling trapped in the present and without fear of taking risks in the future? Picture a tank of lobsters at your local food market or favorite restaurant. In one corner there is a small, one-pound lobster. In the middle there is a large five- or six-pounder slowly making its way across the tank. How did he do it? How did he grow that large? The shell didn't grow but the lobster did. Each time the crustacean felt cramped, restricted, or trapped in his shell, he shed it. He left the safety of the armor that protected him from his environment and his natural enemies. For the next six weeks, the lobster faced his world totally vulnerable to the underwater currents that could bash him against the rocks and to fish that might make him their next meal. During that time he slowly grew a new hard shell that not only provided him with protection but also afforded him ample room to grow. During the first year of his life, he repeated that process six or seven times. In later years he faces the same ordeal twice every year. It is the price he must pay to live and to grow.

Kathie didn't learn the lobster lesson until she was thirty-nine. She is a very attractive woman who has been engaged twice, but in both instances she broke off the engagement prior to the wedding. She grew up as an only child in a financially well-to-do family. Her father worked as an engineer. His earnings were steady and he could have supported his family rather comfortably. However, they lived far beyond his salary, because her mother had a substantial trust fund left by her grandfather, who had vast real estate and oil interests. Kathie's father was able to enjoy the tangible benefits of wealth—a big house, fancy cars and a country club membership, which he cherished—but internally he paid a terrible price. He was emotionally restricted, said little, often appeared lost in his own thoughts, and only seemed happy on the golf course. His relationship with his wife was considerate but distant. In everything, he went though the motions but never experienced the emotions.

Kathie's mother was the stereotypical debutante, a Junior League member and a charity ball sponsor. She was cold, rigid, coiffed to the last hair and always the lady. Beneath the surface, however, was an angry woman with a cutting tongue, ice water in her veins and an insincere heart. She never bothered to get to know her daughter. The nanny took care of that. All she really wanted was a showpiece, a child to complete the picture of a perfect family. As long as Kathie performed to perfection in school, at church, and in her myriad activities, everything was copacetic.

Kathie met all of these expectations. Even as a child she was exceptional. She was slender, athletic, well-mannered and talented. She excelled in ballet, was a better than average swimmer, had outstanding artistic ability and was always a lady. Mother was constantly told what wonderful a daughter she had raised, and Kathie felt obligated to uphold that standard. She was never allowed to be a child, to fail, to trip, to spill, or otherwise demonstrate human frailties or emotions. Kathie was never permitted to be real. When she first came to my office, she was the outward picture of perfection. In my notes I jotted down "Strong on form and weak in substance." Not only was it difficult for her to come to my office, it was almost impossible for her to verbalize why she was there. She was vague to the point that her words seemed directed primarily toward telling me why she shouldn't be there. She had everything in life—position, talent, beauty and wealth—but her physician had insisted she make the appointment.

Four or five sessions later, it became evident how miserable she really was. Most of her symptoms were physiological in nature, a cough that appeared during periods of stress, a gagging reflex which often made it difficult to swallow, and her throat closing up in the middle of a conversation for no apparent reason. In her own words, "It is like there is something inside churning and boiling in my chest, but I can't let anything inside to quell it or let it out to rid myself of it."

Without realizing it, she was accurately diagnosing her own condition. Her emotions were trapped inside herself. She was furious about the boundaries she had accepted early in her life. At the same time, it was too painful to recognize her own anger. After all, she had been taught well; a lady of proper standing would never express anger and hostility outwardly. She was periodically having to swallow, literally and figuratively, any expression of negative, disagreeable, or unacceptable emotions.

Figuratively speaking, her shell was cracking and it took the persuasion of a caring physician who, despite her objections, referred her to my office. In therapy, she was given the emotional support, permission and courage to leave her past behind and to grow a new covering that she could wear equally attractively but far more comfortably.

There is an important lesson that all of us can learn from Kathie and from the lobster. In the course of living, some of us paint ourselves into tight corners. We construct vocational and behavioral paths, which we pursue for years only to find ourselves eventually feeling stifled, burned out, and trapped financially, professionally and emotionally. Some of us discover that the career path we chose many years ago no longer holds the enchantment it once did, or we might realize that the marketplace that once provided us a living has radically changed. However, even with reality staring us straight in the face, we can feel too paralyzed to effect a change. In some cases, the city or state in which we once wanted to live out our days, no longer seems safe or enjoyable, but we are too fearful to make a move. Even worse, our marriages, our life styles, and the emotional patterns we have carved out over the years may now seem restrictive, cramped, and painful. The solutions are many. We can tolerate it; make the best of it; get drunk or drugged, overeat, stay depressed, blame others, leave, run away, self-destruct—or learn a lesson from a lobster.

Lesson 1: When our present circumstances start to squeeze, we can choose to grow. Recognize that we have choices in life. We can decide to complain. We can stay stagnant until we are squeezed to death by our own state of paralysis, or we can choose to grow. But growth isn't easy. It takes more than words. Playing the victim, blaming others, and other forms of denial are all counterproductive to growth. To grow we must decide to run toward reality, not away from it.

Lesson 2: Ask yourself, "Do I want to stay a one-pounder for the rest of my life?" If your answer is "No," you have little choice but to run toward your fears. Although it is terrifying and dangerous to shed the old shell, we must. No matter if our shell is a dominating attitude, a sharp tongue, passive-aggressive behavior, or self-destructive actions. To get where we want to be, the old shell has to go.

Lesson 3: If it doesn't work, drop it or change it. Leave behind your old rigid behaviors and beliefs. Cast aside the safety of the easy, the comfortable and the familiar. That means being truly open to new ideas. Despite our fears, it begs us to be emotionally at risk. We need to have the courage of our convictions, to honestly speak our minds without malice or hostility, and to confront both old and new challenges in life.

Lesson 4: Shedding our old shells doesn't necessarily mean leaving, quitting, divorcing, or running off to some new escape. Quite the contrary. Before we make any major changes or decisions, we first scrutinize our motivations to determine whether our discontent with others really stems from dissatisfaction with ourselves.

Lesson 5: We did not get where we are in life by accident. In most cases, we are trapped in shells of our own making. But similar to the molting lobster, we can shed old behavioral patterns. We are capable of developing new and better means of coping, which helps us feel secure within ourselves and open us to future growth.

Lesson 6: The material for growth most often comes from within. Disregarding everything we ever experienced, learned, or developed in the past does not rid us of our ills or guarantee a new future. We must come to value who and what we are on the inside. That means recognizing our special capabilities, forgiving our perceived weaknesses, and accepting what we cannot change. Remember that after shedding its shell, the lobster doesn't turn into a sturgeon, he just becomes a bigger, better lobster. The same can be said about us if we crack our shells in order to grow.

Lesson 7: The meat inside can be sweet and desirable to others. If we have the courage to open our hard shells and make our inner selves vulnerable to those we love and to those we want to love us, our confidence in our worth will grow.

It is only through accepting ourselves that we are ever able to share ourselves with others. An honest display of self forms the basis for true intimacy. Intimacy supplies a solid foundation for a world where new ideas can unfold and new directions can materialize. All this is possible only if we have the willpower to make ourselves vulnerable to others. Ask any lobster. He will tell you that you must let go to grow.

Steamed or Oven-Roasted Lobster

If you don't live in Maine or one of the adjoining coastal states, serving up a lobster dinner may seem a formidable task. Try to overcome that attitude. Most supermarkets around the country carry live lobsters ready for the cooking, and it's easy if you're open or receptive to it. It makes for an elegant presentation that belies how little effort it requires.

1 live lobster per person
Lots of melted butter
Lemon wedges

I prefer steamed to boiled lobster because it is far less messy in terms of the dripping water after it is cooked. All it takes is a very large pot of salted boiling water about 2 to 3 inches deep, a bed of seaweed on the bottom, a wire rack or pasta strainer deep enough to allow you to plunge the lobsters in head first. Cover and return water to boil about 10 minutes for a 1-1/4 to 1-1/2 pound lobster. Split body and claws and serve immediately with butter and lemon.

If you prefer it baked, it only requires two or three additional ingredients and a lack of squeamishness.

1/4 cup Italian bread crumbs
1 tablespoon chopped Italian parsley
1/2 stick (4 tablespoons) butter
1/4 teaspoon seasoned salt
1/4 teaspoon minced garlic
2 teaspoons lemon juice

Place lobsters, shell side up, on a board and plunge a chef's knife blade facing the head, into the point where the tail meets the body and forms a sort of "T." This severs the spinal cord and instantly kills the lobster. However, it will continue to move due to muscle reflexes. To avoid this experience, place the live lobsters in a freezer for 10 to 15 minutes before severing their spine. It numbs them and you can proceed with splitting them with far less difficulty. Crack the claws, turn lobster on its back and split in half lengthwise without cutting through the back shell. Butterfly, then remove the sack from behind the head and the lungs. Placing a wooden skewer up one side of the split lobster tail will inhibit curling during cooking and enhance the serving appearance. Arrange lobsters on foil-covered cookie sheet. Melt butter, add bread crumbs and mix until they begin to brown. Add parsley, minced garlic, lemon juice and salt and pepper to taste. Sprinkle evenly over body and tail meat. Roast until tail meat is opaque and bread crumbs are crisp, approximately 12 to 15 minutes. Serve with lemon wedges.

Hint: The best time of year to buy and serve lobsters is in early spring when their shells are hard and full of meat.

Chapter 17

Roasted Tomatoes and Caramelized Kids

❊ ❊ ❊ ❊ ❊ ❊ ❊ ❊ ❊ ❊ ❊ ❊ ❊ ❊ ❊

It was the second time in a month that I had opened the door of my high-rise apartment to let the firemen in. They were fully equipped in their fire-fighting gear, complete with axes in hand. They wanted to investigate the source of the smoke that had permeated the hallway and triggered the fire alarm. On both occasions, the firemen found it difficult to believe I was deliberately "burning" Roma tomato halves. I tried to describe the recipe to them but it fell on deaf ears. They finally left, but only after they were fully convinced that the lunatic in #420 wasn't going to burn down the building. The remainder of the week, the concierge staff, the security people and the porters all gave me curious looks, as if to say, "Why not just admit that you goofed? After all, burning dinner isn't a criminal offense."

The firemen and the building staff weren't interested, but let me tell you that the recipe for these tomatoes is really unique. It requires that you first sauté the tomatoes face down in a very hot skillet on the highest heat until they caramelize. The goal is to turn them so black that they appear and even smell almost burned. They are then placed face up in a baking dish, topped with various spices and herbs and put into a 400 degree oven for 20 to 30 minutes. From this description, even I find it hard to believe how truly wonderful they are. Of course, the real proof lies in the eating. The tomatoes are mild, very sweet and have a rich taste too difficult to fully describe in words.

It seems almost paradoxical that we need to subject tomatoes to such harsh treatment to achieve these delicious results. But it works! The trick is knowing how much is enough. Too little heat and you never obtain the intense flavor of the tomato along with its natural sweetness. Too much fire and the sugars burn instead of caramelizing, and then, of course, the tomatoes need to be tossed out. The whole procedure requires that you first have a love for tomatoes. Second, you must be willing to exert the effort required to elicit and then enhance the tomato's inherent flavor. Finally, you must agree that the end result is worth the energy needed to clean up the mess you make in the process.

I see a great deal of similarity between the steps necessary to complete this recipe and the rearing of children. For example, if you want kids in your life, you need to love them and value them. If you're not willing to do the work, it's a mistake to include them on your menu. Forget what others think or what they want for you. It is your kitchen and you are the one who will have to expend the energy required to help make your kids successes

Too many times I have seen responsible, conscientious individuals in therapy, who truly want the best for their children but, if the truth were known, they never really wanted children to begin with. The end result is they go through the motions of raising children, but without the necessary fire of emotions, and the fullness of flavor never quite develops in their kids. These children grow up lacking spice, individuality, confidence and character. They go through life knowing the names of their feelings but rarely expressing or experiencing the depth of their emotions. At some level of awareness the children know they've been cheated, even when the parents cannot admit it to themselves.

The flip side to cool indifference is when we abuse our kids through excess heat. We condition them for behavior that is too passive, too cooperative, too loud, too rebellious or too negative. No matter the mode of expression, their behavior is excessive because excess is the only means they have of shouting, sometimes silently, for the emotional involvement they so desperately desire.

Children, like tomatoes, possess an inherent goodness or sweetness that you, the parent, can either develop and reinforce or silence and squelch. It is no different from the chef who wants to serve carrots with the entrée but has yet to decide whether to serve them with a candy glaze or a splash of tart vinegar. Unlike the chef, however, most parents decide how to raise their children based on unconscious factors made up of covert feelings of anger, guilt, and resentment. For example, imagine a man who married a woman because she was pregnant. He thought it was the right thing to do. Years later, he blames the child for his being trapped in the marriage. He then uses that child as a dumping ground for his own anger. His behavior is common to numerous mothers or fathers I have seen. They strongly resent and are often jealous of the emotions directed by their spouse toward a chosen child rather than toward them. I have frequently seen guilt manifest itself in situations involving divorced fathers. They often over-indulge their children and lavish them with expensive gifts or trips that they can ill afford. If they have remarried, their new spouses strongly resent these behaviors. I cannot begin to count how many second marriages I have seen go to the divorce courts because of the emotional power struggle between a new spouse and children from a previous marriage.

Another example that comes to mind is that of a highly intelligent, and otherwise successful divorced father who was a rank amateur when it came to dealing with his offspring. In one glaring instance, he offered to give his son a new Ford Explorer as a high school graduation gift. His son refused it. Nothing short of a four-wheel drive Jeep Eagle would do. Against the advice of his new wife, he capitulated.

Although he claimed to feel comfortable with his decision, there was a sudden and radical change in his attitude and behavior toward his wife. Following one particularly explosive interaction she asked him why he seemed so sad, he screamed, "You are selfish, uncaring, and manipulative! You are only after my money and you better learn how to treat kids with love if you ever expect to have any of your own with me." It doesn't take a Ph.D. in psychology to recognize that, after giving in to his son, this father became emotionally depressed. However, he couldn't kick his own backside and he felt too guilty for divorcing his family to stand up to his son. Consequently, he directed his anger toward his new wife.

With another man, I saw the gift of a new car to his daughter on her sixteenth birthday result in months, even years, of misdirected anger toward the girl. Obviously, the father never wanted to buy the car in the first place. He was buying the love he feared he lost when he divorced the girl's mother. He was guilty, but he was also resentful and angry.

As a result, he often lost his temper and issued ridiculous ultimatums.

Both fathers hated themselves for their inability to set limits or to say no. They had little confidence that they were worthy of love, and had no concept of when enough is enough.

Too much fire and too little heat both end up with negative results. We must learn to moderate the degree of heat that we bring to bear on our children and on our tomatoes. Each one has its own individual characteristics and thus may require different treatment. Large tomatoes take longer to cook than small ones. More aggressive children may require more heat than passive ones. But all children require a mixture of sensitivity, warmth, and a pinch of sugar. In deciding how much is enough, we need to establish boundaries or limits to direct our own actions and feelings. Boundaries let our children know what we expect of them and how far they can and cannot go.

Here's a story that a patient in therapy told me about her mother. On the negative side, Carol's mother was emotionally cold and didn't demonstrate or verbally express affection. On the positive side, she was very clear about what she expected from Carol and what she was willing to do in return. Carol told me that her twenty-seven-year-old, recently married son decided to move to his grandmother's hometown. He and his wife went to Grandma and asked if they could live with her for approximately six months. During that time they both planned to work and save their money, which they would then apply toward renting a place of their own. Grandma's answer was firm. "I'll think it over and let you know tomorrow." The following day, she said, "Okay. It is not something I necessarily want, but something I am willing to do to help you out. You have six

months to work, to save, to keep me company, and
then to leave."

A day later, they moved in, complete with clothing,
two articles of furniture, a bed they stored in the garage, a
bowl of tropical fish and their dog. One week later,
Grandma came home to find a new arrival in the house, a
cute, playful little puppy who seemed immediately attracted
to her and particularly excited by the pompoms on her
slippers. She had no particular resentment toward this
puppy, but for her, things were clear cut. She told her
grandson, "I said you could move in the way you were for
six months. Today, when I arrived home there was a new
addition that wasn't in our bargain. It's up to you to
determine what you are going to do. The puppy is adorable
but that has nothing to do with our bargain. You can choose
to return the puppy wherever you got it, or you, the puppy
and your other dog can leave."

Carol was amazed by her son's response. He wasn't
angry. He didn't object or try to convince or cajole or
change his grandmother's mind. Shortly thereafter, he left
with the puppy in hand. More importantly, however, is that
his grandmother never needed to get angry, feel guilty, or
become resentful. Why? Because she gave thought to what
she was willing to do. Grandma knew where she stood. She
didn't say "yes" to anything she would resent later. She
didn't respond in vague terms like "maybe" or "perhaps or
if things change, then we'll see." When you dealt with
Grandma, you knew where she stood, and consequently you
knew where you stood. What a comfort it must be to live in
a world where the rules are clearly stated, where people
don't interact with hidden agendas and need not misdirect
or punish one another because they resent themselves and
their inability to set limits or say "no." No wonder Carol's

son didn't argue or try to bargain. He knew that he was free to make his own decision but he had clear-cut choices: get rid of the puppy or give up the opportunity to save money for a six-month period. Because Grandma was forthright, she didn't have a big mess to clean up after every interaction. She practiced tough love and it worked.

For me, the similarity between caramelizing tomatoes and raising kids is rather straightforward. You have to start out with a love for both of them. You need to set limits on how you deal with them. You can't apply too much heat, nor can you be too cool. You have to be careful in the application of fire not to singe or burn them. You have to be willing to add some spices, a little dab of olive oil, a large pinch of sugar and a whole lot of your attention, time and energy. The end result? You will have wonderfully tasty tomatoes and highly lovable kids. Delectable kids are a treat that we deserve, and one we can have if we possess sufficient courage to give of ourselves to exercise our own good judgment and to be emotionally vulnerable. We must recognize that every child won't respond the same way, but if we practice commitment, care, and concern, our kids will come through it and so will we.

Oven-Roasted Tomatoes

This is a great appetizer or vegetable dish. It can also be mashed and spread on bruschetta, sprinkled with Parmesan cheese then broiled and served with cocktails or pulsed several times in a blender or food processor and used as a wonderful sauce over pasta, either alone or it can be mixed with some well browned cubes of bacon, pancetta or mushrooms for a little heartier sauce.

2 cups extra virgin olive oil
12 firm large plum or Roma tomatoes cored and halved
    lengthwise
sea salt
1/4 cup sugar
2 teaspoons minced garlic
2 teaspoons fresh thyme or 1 teaspoon dried thyme leaves
1/4 cup red wine vinegar
1/4 cup Parmesan cheese (optional)
1/4 cup balsamic vinegar (optional)

Preheat the oven to 400°. Heat oil in a large heavy skillet. Fit as many tomatoes in the pan, cut side down, without being overcrowded. Cook over high heat without moving the tomatoes until they are almost caramelized, approximately 5 to 6 minutes. If you have a screen to cover the skillet with, it will help control the splattering. Do not worry if the tomatoes appear to be burned, it is just the natural sugar darkening. Remove tomatoes carefully with a spatula to a glass or ceramic baking dish large enough to hold all the tomato halves cooked side up. Repeat this procedure until all tomatoes are cooked. Sprinkle with sugar. Additional oil may be necessary. Add garlic for one minute to cooking juices in skillet on medium high heat, add red wine vinegar and de-glaze pan. Pour mixture of cooking juices, garlic and vinegar over the tomatoes in baking pan. Season lightly with sea salt, fresh ground pepper, and thyme leaves. Bake the tomatoes in the middle of the oven until browned and sizzling, about 30 minutes. Serve hot, warm or at room temperature. Sprinkle with a little Parmesan cheese if desired. For a different touch you can drizzle some balsamic vinegar over the top of the tomatoes when you first remove them from the oven.

Chapter 18

Where's the Beef?

✳ ✳ ✳ ✳ ✳ ✳ ✳ ✳ ✳ ✳ ✳ ✳ ✳ ✳ ✳

"Where's the Beef?" was the punch line in a well known Wendy's TV commercial that criticized the lack of meat in a competitor's hamburger. It implied that double the beef is double the fun. Meanwhile, many dieticians decreed that eating beef increases bad cholesterol and is generally detrimental to our health. "No way" say the experts hired by the Association of American Beef Councils. "We need protein to fuel our bodies." It seems the more we learn, the more confused we become. Sometimes we get to a point where we don't know what side of our bread to butter, which expert to believe or whether an association is concerned with us or only their own self-serving agenda.

It is the same in human relations. There are times when any one of us can feel so low that we doubt whether our friends really care, and question the real reason our spouses claim to love us. Was that joke about getting more life insurance really a joke? Are we too old, too fat, too poor? If we get sick or aren't able to produce, would they still be there? How do you ever know? Sometimes we can reach a point where we doubt if even God cares. If he did, why didn't we win the state lottery, get the promotion, turn out naturally thin and beautiful, or discover that the picture we bought at a flea market for next to nothing is an original Picasso?

I don't know the answer to these questions. I strongly suspect, however, that when we arrive at a place where the whole world looks black and we question the reason for everything, we are probably pretty depressed. During these times, which Winston Churchill called "Black Dog" days, it is difficult to see or experience any joy in life, let alone respond to it. It doesn't necessarily mean that you are in need of therapy or a daily dose of Prozac. These feelings can result from our own physiological or psychological cycle. They may come about because of a prolonged period of sleep deprivation. We may be working too hard, socializing too much or experiencing an extreme amount of personal stress. In some people, depression is associated with an extended period of inclement weather, personal disappointment, or an emotional loss.

On these occasions, the one thing you can be sure of is that life seems something to dread rather than to enjoy. It is a time when old wounds are easily opened, when we revisit past hurts and become acutely sensitive to inner feelings of loneliness and despair. For anyone who has ever experienced one or more of these days, I would like to relate a story that I believe will prove extremely meaningful to you.

Many years ago, I saw a woman in therapy who was depressed, unhappy in her marriage, wanting to leave her family but fearful of going out in the world. Ellen expressed sadness over the prospect of separating her children from their father and guilt over an affair she was

having with the meat department manager in a local supermarket. At the same time, the affair was the only joy in her
life. She described the man as caring, sensitive, and willing
to listen to her.

Ellen and her lover had devised a scheme where,
whenever she shopped for meat, she would select T-bone
steaks, sirloin strips, rib roasts and veal chops, but he
would label the packages as chuck steak or ground beef.
As a result, Ellen's family was indirectly benefitting from
her affair, in a perverse sort of way. They were enjoying
cuts of meat that normally would have been beyond the
family budget.

In therapy, Ellen came to realize that if she was ever
going to resolve her situation, she needed to deal with her
life and the supermarket more honestly. She had to end the
relationship with the butcher and genuinely attempt to
establish a relationship with her husband. I suggested new
ways of reaching out and loving her husband that would
help her invest herself emotionally in her marriage. If, after
expending this effort, she still perceived her spouse as
lacking and her life as empty, she could then make the
decision to get a divorce, but at least she would have made
an honest attempt to work within her present circumstances.
Thus, she would be better able to live with herself, to be a
better mother and to go out and start an honest new life

It took time, along with a great deal of courage on her
part, but she ended the affair. She stopped stealing emotionally from her marriage and stopped stealing T-bones from
the grocery store too. She started to feel better about herself.
She even began to think that there might be a possibility of
improving and even enjoying her marriage.

Then, four or six weeks after she ended her affair, she
and her husband had a large altercation. He carried on at

length about all of her deficiencies, most notably the prolonged period of sexual abstinence—which he admitted had changed of late—and her lack of interest in the home— at least in the past. To make matters worse, he added, "I don't know what is going on around here. I'm beginning to think that you're socking money away so you can leave. I used to get T-bones, strip steaks, rib roasts and veal chops. Now, I'm working just as hard, taking the same amount of overtime, but lately all I get is Hamburger Helper. Where's the beef?"

Of course, he had no way of knowing that the change in his diet was something he should be thankful for. It is the same way in many aspects of our lives. Often we are blind to the good things that come our way, because they aren't obvious or on the surface. We are usually quick to find fault, to criticize and lament, instead of looking beneath the veneer and counting our blessings.

On a more personal level, not long ago, our son was at the head of a waiting list for a dual transplant of a kidney and pancreas. Physically, he was in extremely bad shape, and he was totally depressed emotionally. His senses were dulled, and he was unable to carry on even an average conversation. Though he was on dialysis, we feared he would die before suitable organs became available.

Then one day, out of the blue, he received a call from his transplant coordinator saying that a kidney and pancreas were available. He rushed to the hospital for a final evaluation to ensure that he was strong enough physically to survive the operation and to permit the new organs to live. In a devastating turn of events, the radiologist noticed a spot on one of my son's lungs. He was unsure whether it was a growth, an infection, cancer, or even tuberculosis.

In order to make a definitive diagnosis, they took him into surgery. They cut open several ribs, collapsed his lung, and took a biopsy in order to see what treatment, if any, was needed. In the meantime, the available organs were given to someone else.

For the next month, he went through an inordinate amount of pain and discomfort. Once again, in light of his weakened condition, we had little hope that he would survive. Fortunately, the spot on his lung proved to be only a foreign body, which he had breathed in and which was now embedded in his lung tissue. The spot was something of no medical consequence but its discovery had caused him to lose the available organs. It had also led to an unnecessary operation, a considerable amount of pain, and a period of healing before he would once again be eligible for a transplant—when and if a new donor could be found.

After a time, another set of compatible organs became available, and my son was able to receive a new kidney and pancreas. We feel blessed. He is physically well, intellectually alert, working for the first time in years and looking like his old self. Even more, his attitude has changed. His values are different and he appreciates the little things in life, such as being able to eat a piece of cake, waking up in the morning with energy and not having to be connected to a tube each night to artificially clean his body fluids.

Another twist in the story came to light about four months after my son's transplant. David found out that the organs he had originally been scheduled to receive, the ones we had desperately grieved losing, turned out to have been so traumatized during the death of the donor that they failed to thrive. Sadly, the individuals who received the liver and the heart from this donor both died. The person who received the kidney and pancreas intended for my son is still alive, and is back on the waiting list for another set of organs. The recipient of the other kidney was fortunate to receive a second transplant and appears to be doing well.

Prior to this discovery, there was no way to see that David's loss was in fact a blessing. It was not something to be bitter over. It was instead something to have been thankful for. We have all learned to be grateful through this experience and to savor the value of each new day.

Above all else, this experience reinforced my earlier belief that whenever our world seems empty or hopeless, our despair does not necessarily reflect the entire story. All of us can have Black Dog days, but as trite as it may sound, we must try to make lemonade out of our lemons. Despite the tragic outcome for some of the transplant recipients, each one had made an important decision to move forward in the hope that something good was just ahead.

To choose to persevere and to move forward requires that we look objectively at our own pattern of behavior. We have to ask ourselves, how often do we experience Black Dog days? Is it once every four to six weeks, every three or four months, or once a year? If these bouts are occasional, we must accept that no one's life is 100 percent happy. Down days are part of living. If these bad times are occurring more and more often, however, or becoming more severe with each occurrence, I strongly suggest that you seek professional help. But if we experience periodic or random downturns, we needn't fight the problem, run from it, or try to cure it. We can never outrun it or hide from it permanently anyway. Neither should we try to drink, drug, eat, sleep or screw our way to mental health or emotional happiness. Instead, we must learn to float with the tide. It is not a major crime to cry, stay in bed for a whole day or pull the covers over our heads and feel sorry for ourselves. But when we do, we cannot punish ourselves for it. You, me, every one of us is entitled to a couple of down days without feeling or creating additional pain or guilt for ourselves. On some occasions, we may emotionally need or deserve the respite. Remember, the world isn't a perfect place. Sometimes it dishes up things that aren't happy or joyful.

One word of caution might be necessary. Whenever we feel low, we must not make any major personal, professional or business decisions. That means, when you hit the emotional skids, don't quit your job, confront your boss, colleagues, spouse or kids. Don't see a lawyer about a divorce, impulsively decide to get married, or consider ending your life. Remember that each of these behaviors is a rather permanent solution to what, I believe, you will later discover is only a temporary problem or state of being.

After we have sufficiently indulged ourselves emotionally, we need make a conscious decision about how long we intend to be depressed, whether it be for three hours, two days, or until the beginning of the weekend. This recommendation may seem utterly crazy, but believe me, we do decide, albeit unconsciously, how long we intend to stay angry, not communicate, avoid physical closeness, or push our lover away. What I am suggesting is that we take conscious control of an otherwise unconscious decision, and thereby take greater responsibility for our lives.

Once you've made the decision, by all means bask in the sadness and despair for the period you have allotted. (Yes, the absurdity may occasionally overtake you and hasten your recovery.) But when it's over, it's time to hit the floor running. We must take the necessary steps, even if they are baby steps, to get to where we want to go. We might shower, indulge our body, get a manicure, a facial or a haircut, dress up in something special or call a friend for lunch. We could give ourselves a gift, do something for ourselves that we have wanted to do, or buy something we didn't think we deserved. We might also set up an exercise schedule, start eating more wisely and getting sufficient sleep. In all, we need to start taking good care of ourselves.

Lastly, we must try to look beneath the surface of the words and deeds of others. This is the most difficult part of all, particularly when we feel alone in the world or uncared for. But we may well discover that our loved ones, in fact, care very deeply about us, although they may not articulate it well. In the process, we may learn that others can't always meet our emotional needs and standards, but we can help them to do better. Sometimes it requires that we spell out very clearly what is troubling us. We may have to draw pictures to get our message across. We need to learn to "ask for," not demand, the things we think will help us to feel better. Many of us were told early in life that "if we have to ask for it, it ain't worth having." Well, I am here to tell you, that is pure bunk. If it is worth having, it is most certainly worth asking for.

On the other side of the coin, we must look to our loved ones, families, institutions, and charities to see if there is something we can do to help them. No matter how low we feel, there is always someone we can give to, who in turn might be able to give back to us. More often than not, what we put in is what we get back, the more we invest, the greater the return. If we are physically well and have the wherewithal, it is in our own best interest to do something for others. In the long run, we will be the beneficiaries. Moreover, by coming in touch with our feelings of helplessness and aloneness we may also become more compassionate, more sensitive, more empathetic toward others and more confident in ourselves.

The truth that we can be blind to the good within us and around us is best described by Antoine de St. Exupery in *The Little Prince.* In the story, the little prince meets a sly fox, who agrees to share his most precious secret with him. The secret, he said, is that "It is only with the heart that one can see rightly; what is essential is invisible to the eye." Perhaps we all need to see that there is far more beef available in life than ever meets the eye.

Eggplant Parmigiana

Where's the beef might be an appropriate question when you serve this dish, because adding meat is optional. Either way, it can easily serve as a main course. Serve it with a salad and warm garlic bread, and I guarantee that no one will leave the table feeling hungry. It can also be served as an antipasto or as a vegetable side dish.

4 medium eggplants, about 4 pounds
salt
vegetable oil for frying
1 cup unbleached all purpose flour
3 tablespoons extra virgin olive oil
4 garlic cloves, peeled and left whole
4 cups canned imported Italian plum tomatoes, with their
     juice, crushed slightly
1 teaspoon sugar
3/4 pound thinly sliced fresh mozzarella
1 cup freshly grated Parmigiana-Reggiano cheese
1 bunch fresh basil
1 lb. ground hamburger or sausage (optional)

Preheat oven to 350°.

Peel the eggplant and cut lengthwise into 1/4 inch slices. Place slices in a large colander and sprinkle with salt. Let stand 30 minutes. The salt will draw out any of the eggplant's bitter juices. Drain on paper towels.

Heat 1 inch of oil in a large skillet over medium heat. Coat the eggplant slices lightly with flour and slip as many of them as will fit comfortably at one time into the hot oil. Cook until they are golden on both sides, about 2 minutes. Repeat with remaining eggplant slices and drain.

Heat olive oil in a small saucepan over medium heat. Add the garlic cloves and let them turn a golden brown, then discard them. Add the tomatoes, roughly crushed and sprinkled with seasoned salt and sugar. As soon as the tomatoes come to a boil, reduce the heat to low and simmer, stirring occasionally for 6-8 minutes, or until the sauce has a medium thick consistency.

Spread a thin layer of sauce on the bottom of a 9 x 12 baking dish, and cover with a layer of fried eggplant slices, slightly overlapping each other. Spread some more sauce over the eggplant, cover with a layer of mozzarella and about 6 torn basil leaves. Sprinkle top with Parmigiana. Repeat with one more layer of eggplant, tomatoes, mozzarella, basil and Parmigiana.

Add a final layer of eggplant, and sauce, and sprinkle with Parmigiana and Mozzarella. Place the dish in the oven and bake 30 to 35 minutes. Remove from oven and let the eggplant settle for 20 to 25 minutes before serving.

Chapter 19

Plain Vanilla

❊ ❊ ❊ ❊ ❊ ❊ ❊ ❊ ❊ ❊ ❊ ❊ ❊ ❊ ❊

It was really no big deal, just one of those disagreements any two people trying to live together go through. In fact, I've long since forgotten what it was about, but I suspect I'll always recall how it ended. What I do remember is that, in the course of our verbal exchange, I became "justifiably" exasperated by Harriet's lack of logic and her inability to see my point of view, and I said, "That's crazy; you're worse than any one of my patients."

Her answer stopped me in my tracks. "What do you want, plain vanilla? Because that's not me and I don't want to be that."

I hardly knew what to say. So instead of saying anything, I turned her question over in my mind. *Do I want a plain vanilla lover, who will always agree with me, never cause me grief, and who is passively pleasant all the time?*

The answer wasn't difficult. *Of course not!* I'm the guy who rarely drives home the same way two nights in a row. I'll eat vanilla ice cream, but only when I can mix it with berries of some type or top it with chocolate or caramel syrup. Plain vanilla is always the same. Sometimes the predictable isn't bad, but over the long haul you can get tired of vanilla, become bored with vanilla. Plain vanilla rarely speaks its mind or makes a statement. Like wallpaper, it just hangs around. I want a life partner who has some spice, some humor, and something that is uniquely "her." There's no question that I want more than plain vanilla out of life, and I suspect you do too.

But let's be honest. The ice cream paddle scoops both ways. Ask yourself the question, "Am I a plain vanilla lover? Do I go blandly through life, choosing dishonest love over making waves?" I've devised a test that will help you see what you are, help you to determine whether something needs altering, and motivate you to initiate that change.

Answer the following questions. Have your partner take the test for you while you take it for him. That way, each of you can see how your partner perceives the way you love compared to your own perceptions. Comparing your answers could help you discover the ways in which you're a fraudulent lover, and pinpoint unrewarding behaviors that you need to alter or eliminate.

1. Are you insecure and defer to your lover's every wish?

2. Do you seek his/her constant approval?

3. Do you avoid saying what you truly think and instead try to say what you think your partner would like you to say?

4. Do you "buy" love by doing things you don't really want to do?

5. Do you do more for others than they could ever do in return?

6. Do you agree with others rather than voice your own opinion?

7. Do you feel ignored if your spouse or date indulges in a long conversation with a member of the opposite sex?

8. Are you jealous and bristle when your partner touches or hugs someone else?

9. Do you resent the attention your partner directs toward someone else when you think it's more intense than the attention directed toward you?

10. Do you pout and use the silent treatment when you feel unloved?

11. Do you refuse to join in potentially enjoyable activities in an effort to create guilt in others?

12. Is sex satisfying to the point that you agree to have it even when you don't want to?

13. In intimate situations, including sexual activity, do you find it difficult to ask for what you want your partner to give you?

14. Do you harbor resentment, resulting in nagging your partner about inconsequential behavior (forgetting to turn off the light, picking up clothes, putting the cap on the toothpaste)?

15. Do you hold on to angry feelings long after the conflict itself is forgotten?

16. Are you embarrassed by the way your partner behaves in public or at social gatherings?

17. Do you tend to keep score and ruminate on and on about past wrongs or indiscretions by your partner?

18. Do you keep a list of old transgressions that you pull out to stifle your partner whenever you argue or disagree?

19. Do you harbor resentment for which you feel you can never forgive your partner?

20. Are you controlling? Do you threaten separation or divorce whenever your partner says things that you don't

want to consider or face?

21. Have you ever physically abused, hit or pushed your partner?

22. Do you demand to make the ultimate decision on every important issue?

23. Do you feel isolated and unneeded when your partner is successful?

24. Do you feel stronger and more essential to the relationship when your partner is weak or having problems?

25. Do you find work to do or become sleepy or otherwise preoccupied when there is a real opportunity for togetherness?

To some degree, all of us are fraudulent lovers. Most of us indulge, to varying degrees, in some of the behaviors described here. But if you answered "Yes" to fifteen or more questions, consider the possibility that you are your own worst enemy in intimate relationships.

Loving behaviors, both constructive and destructive, are learned early in childhood. They stay with us throughout life. Each of us has early loving experiences to learn from, but these aren't always positive or conducive to closeness and intimacy.

These questions weren't designed to find fault but to raise your awareness of the ways that you interact with those you love. Remember, the point of any relationship questionnaire is to help you communicate better and improve your relationships. Don't use it to indict one another. Although few of us escape the learned affliction of fraudulent loving, we all have to recognize that some of the behaviors we learned in our youth may well be destructive in adulthood. The bottom line is this: Some of our so-called loving behaviors probably need changing or improvement.

Why do I call this fraudulent loving? When you love in such a way that you prostitute your own identity, behave in ways that differ from the way you feel, allow people to hurt you to gain their affection, or are reluctant to stand up because you fear rejection, you can't help but grow to resent or even hate the very people you want to love. This resentment may not manifest itself overtly; it may exist in a highly unconscious or underlying fashion. Either way, though, these feelings will eventually make themselves known through hostile behaviors that manifest themselves either overtly, or through passive-aggressive behavior. When you resent the people you love, you express your love in fraudulent ways. The degree to which you sell yourself short to obtain love is the degree to which you are dishonest in your intimate relationships.

Real loving requires that you say to your partner what you genuinely feel; that you share emotions and feelings and opinions and observations honestly; that you risk potential rejection, disapproval or disagreement.

People who love one another don't have to think the same thing, believe the same thing, or behave the same way. In fact, when you really think about it, living with a carbon copy of yourself would be pretty dull. Living with someone who has differing opinions and thoughts and viewpoints makes life more interesting and more challenging.

Now, whenever I find myself engaged in an almighty struggle to convince Harriet of the ultimate truth about a controversial issue or position, I try to remember her question, "What do you want, plain vanilla?" I can't help but smile, because that is the last thing I want in life. I want the interest and the spark and the excitement of living with someone who contributes new viewpoints and new energy into our relationship.

Take the test for yourself and take it again for your partner. Have your partner do the same. When you're both finished, discuss your answers, and you may discover that you don't want plain vanilla, either.

Mashed Potatoes Three Ways

Mashed potatoes probably the most widely accepted comfort food that satisfies both children and adults. They're plain vanilla in color and often taste bland as well, but they don't have to. This basic food can be dressed up and served as a classic addition to a formal dinner.

I   Garlic Mashed Potatoes

4 lbs. small red potatoes, unpeeled, or Yukon Gold
       potatoes, quartered.
8 cloves garlic, smashed
2 teaspoons salt
1 cup chicken stock
seasoned salt and freshly ground pepper to taste
4 tablespoons butter
2 teaspoons paprika
2 tablespoons grated Parmesan cheese

1. Place the potatoes in a medium sized pot and cover with cold water. Add garlic and 1 teaspoon salt. Bring to a boil. Boil for 15-20 minutes, or until potatoes are tender.

2. Drain the potatoes and garlic and return them to pot.

3. Add the stock, 4 tablespoons of butter, salt and pepper to taste.

4. Whip all ingredients together.

Serves 8

II   Garlic Mashed Potatoes with Roquefort and
Parmesan Cheese.

1/3 cup Roquefort cheese
2 cup grated Parmesan cheese

Add to Garlic Mashed Potatoes (see recipe above) and
mix with an electric mixer.

III   Garlic Mashed Potatoes with Caramelized Onions.

2 tablespoons butter
1 tablespoon olive oil
2 teaspoons salt
2 red onions peeled and sliced thin
3 teaspoons brown sugar
4 tablespoons chicken stock

1. Heat large skillet over medium heat. Add oil and
butter. When hot, add onions and salt and cook until soft,
stirring occasionally.
2. After approximately 20 minutes, turn heat down to
low and stir in sugar and chicken stock. Cook until stock is
reduced—about 10 minutes.
3. Mix browned, caramelized onions with garlic
mashed potatoes (see recipe above) and wait for your
family or guests to squeal with delight.

Chapter 20

Life Is a Piece of Cake

❈ ❈ ❈ ❈ ❈ ❈ ❈ ❈ ❈ ❈ ❈ ❈ ❈ ❈ ❈

One of my favorite things is the smell of chocolate cake fresh out of the oven. Within minutes the rich, sweet aroma permeates the entire house. Invariably, I must admit, my inner child immediately takes over. I know better than to try to cut a cake while it is still hot, but the little kid in me sometimes forgets.

One afternoon, as the deliciously familiar fragrance filled the kitchen, the little boy inside my head shouted, "Go for it!" He wasn't interested in reason or facts, and he was far too impatient to wait for the cake to cool down.

"You deserve it," he said. "Just take a deep breath and imagine an ice cold glass of milk and a piece of chocolate cake hot from the oven." I had to admit that it would taste good.

"Don't worry. Just use a serrated knife and cut it large enough so it won't fall apart." *Yeah, just cut it large enough...*

"Go ahead. Cut it. This is gonna be great!"

Have you ever tried to cut a piece of hot cake? If so, you know it doesn't cut. It crumbles. It collapses into ragged, unequal pieces that even all the king's horses and all the king's men can't put together again. It's hard to be discreet when you cut a hot cake.

Had I exercised more restraint, I could have waited for that cake to cool. I might still have used the serrated knife, but I would have ended up with a cleanly cut, beautiful to behold and wonderful to eat piece of cake.

All it would have taken was some good common sense and a wee bit of patience; but far too often, we don't wait. Instead, we listen to the urgings of an emotional seven- or eight-year-old. Why? Do we not have common sense? Or do we just not use the common sense we have?

Cutting a cake is one thing, but I've watched intelligent, successful adults act like immature, impulsive little children, using absolutely no common sense in every imaginable kind of situation and relationship. And not just once. More often than not, we repeat the same mistakes over and over throughout our lives.

Oddly enough, these ill-chosen behavioral patterns occur primarily in our most intimate relationships. We act in ways at home that we would never dream to repeat at work or with our friends. When we let our guard down, we stop thinking and we behave with our hearts instead of our heads.

I am not just talking about people who are "sick" or pathological. In relationships that are meaningful and significant, most of us respond the same way. We toss our intellect aside, and our emotional inner child takes over. We feel hurt, ashamed, guilty, threatened, or fearful, and we react accordingly, with behavior that might be expected from an eight-year-old. We explode emotionally, attack physically or verbally, or run away from the person or situation that we perceive to be the source of our pain.

The techniques we use range from rationalization, denial, excessive preoccupation with work, athletics, drugs, alcohol, affairs, cleaning the house, caring for the kids, or walking out the door. Some of us have learned to escape within ourselves. We close up, develop hard exteriors, and push others away. The sad part, however, is that none of these techniques help to resolve our problems. They only serve to sweep them under the carpet; out of sight but not out of mind. The problems continue to work insidiously to slowly erode the positive relationships we could have had with others and with ourselves.

The only solution is to think before we act. To confront the things we fear and to trust our good common sense. These behaviors are rarely taught to us. In fact, they are in sharp contrast to what we learned emotionally during our formative years. We were taught to run from pain and to kill any invader.

Our physical bodies provide us with an example of survival techniques based on fight or flight behavior. However, on occasion, this process can contribute to our own undoing. A good example can be seen in organ transplant operations, where the greatest risk stems from the body rejecting the new organ. In a similar fashion, I have observed patients indulge in emotionally self-destructive rejection behavior all the while recognizing the immaturity of their actions.

Michael was a brilliant businessman who was totally dedicated to his job. In his own words, "My work was my hobby, my career, my love—and the company was my family. We have experienced unbelievable success. When I started with the company five years ago, there were fifteen people, including myself, and now we have almost a thousand."

The problem? Though he was nominated both times, for two years in a row Michael had been overlooked for a special award given by the company. For the entire twelve months between the two awards, his focus had been totally centered on winning the next time. His director had told him what he thought he would have to do to win, and Michael had done it all, plus a great deal more.

He had vowed that, this time, he would gain the recognition he desperately wanted from his superiors and his peers. After his first disappointment, he was able to rationalize. "There's always next year." But after finishing second for the second consecutive year, in his mind there was no use trying again. He could never exert the same amount of energy he had invested the previous two years. His manager had even said that he couldn't have performed any better and that he deserved to win. He was filled with despair, hurt, disappointment, and feelings of betrayal. He was at a loss for what he should do.

Then suddenly, his eight-year-old inner child took over, and *he* knew exactly how to react: "Screw 'em. I will never try again. I will put in my forty hours and go through the motions, but they won't get a chance to hurt my feelings again. I won't talk to or cater to any of those sons of bitches. I don't need them. They don't care and neither do I."

By the time he came to see me, about a month later, he was fully engaged in behaving like a hurt, pouting, discontented and disinterested child. "I can't stop thinking about it all," he said. "I know I'm hurting myself, but I can't seem to care. Instead, I'm angry all the time."

His problem needed to be dealt with on two levels. On the practical level, he needed to recognize that his behavior was indeed immature and that his inner child was in control. He needed to take ownership of how he was responding and regain control of his action. Further, he needed to see that what he was doing was mentally self-destructive and counterproductive to any future advancement on the job. If anything, he was handing ammunition to the powers that be, justifying their decision to give the award to someone else.

I asked him, "Even if you decide to leave the company, is that the image you want to leave behind? That's a decision you need to make consciously, and if your answer is 'Yes,' then by all means diligently persist with your present behavior."

I felt that he needed to direct his energy on an emotional level toward understanding and accepting his hurt little kid. It would help him if he understood the reasons behind his long-term anger and despair. I told him, "If you will let me help you to understand your little guy's reactions, you will be able to help him behave in a more constructive manner. This results in your learning to forgive and love that part of you."

I further assured him that it wouldn't happen overnight or after one therapy session, but that it truly could happen if he wanted. Michael agreed to try, and we began to work on the problem. His anger with himself and consequently toward others abated considerably and there was a decided change in his attitude at work. It will take Michael more time before he fully understands the nature of the hurt and pain that he internalized as a boy, and that he built upon as an adult, but he is engaged in the process of self-discovery that I believe will lead him where he desires to be.

Although Michael's situation seemed to revolve around a work problem, it really was no different from

Mary Jo's dilemma. Her husband had left her for his secretary. At one point, he attempted to reconcile, but her internal child was so devastated that she would have none of it. Eight-year-olds don't respond well to rejection, abandonment and betrayal.

To make matters worse, she focused her energy on trying to punish her husband. She forbade their four children to see their father, talk to him on the phone or spend their court-ordered, bi-monthly visitation with him. Her method was simple. She gave her kids the same message she gave her family and friends: "Choose a side—either mine or his. You're either for me or against me. And if you so much as talk to him, I will have nothing to do with you."

At first, she won a landslide victory. After all, she was the victim, the betrayed wife and the martyr. Unfortunately, two years—and two therapists—later, her self-righteous anger was driving people away. She had given up two of her children, both of whom were now living with her husband, and numerous friends had also "chosen the wrong side." Let me make it very clear that in no way am I condoning what Mary Jo's husband did. His deceitful and unacceptable actions caused a tremendous amount of pain. But what he did does not justify her ongoing crusade to hurt him back, which has served to hurt her children, her friends, and most importantly, herself.

Mary Jo's story may seem radically different from Michael's, but the emotional dynamics are the same. In both cases, the wounded little eight-year-old inside took charge, and their ability to respond as an adult seemed to disappear. They continued to view themselves as victims, which they truly were, but to their own detriment they chose to react to their pain instead of acting in accordance with their desires.

Getting even was more important than getting well. Their actions had the effect of a child in a supermarket who throws a temper tantrum by banging his own head against the floor to get his parent's attention. I suppose it's difficult for an eight-year-old to comprehend that living well is truly the best revenge. Fortunately, Michael is beginning to understand, and I'm hopeful that, somewhere down the road, Mary Jo will realize it as well.

If we ever want to take charge of our lives, we must take the time to think before we act. Thinking can enable us to short-circuit our longstanding and predisposition toward impulsive and defensive behavior. Stopping to think can provide sufficient time to ask ourselves two questions: "What do I want?" and "Is what I'm about to do going to help me reach my goal?" Unlike a crumbly cake, as human beings we *can* put all the pieces in our lives together again. But like the cake hot out of the oven, we would do well to take some time to cool down. Then we must learn to practice, to build our resolve, and to use our good common sense. With those important ingredients, we can make our lives a piece of cake.

Carrot Cake

I know that I used chocolate cake as my example in the preceding story, but if life were a piece of cake and there was only one piece that I could have, it would be a large slice of my daughter's carrot cake. It is absolutely head-over-heels above any other I have ever tasted.

One hint: For several years, my daughter-in-law made a pretty fair imitation but it never quite compared to the original. One day, my daughter asked her, "Did you use Mazola oil?"

"No, is that the secret?"

This recipe calls for Mazola oil and, I don't know why, but ever since that conversation, I can't tell the difference between their cakes. I hope that your cake turns out as well.

2 cups sugar
1-1/2 cup Mazola oil (Hey, it's your decision.)
4 eggs
2 cups flour
1 teaspoon baking soda
2 teaspoons cinnamon
1 teaspoon salt
3 cups grated carrots

Mix sugar and oil, add one egg at a time and beat. Add in flour, soda, salt and cinnamon. Mix in grated carrots. Use 3 greased and floured 9-inch round pans. Pour batter in pans, bake 25 minutes at 350°. Cool before icing.

Icing
8 oz cream cheese
4 ounces margarine or butter
1 box powdered sugar
2 teaspoons vanilla
1 cup chopped walnuts
Add raisins if desired

Let cream cheese and margarine soften at room temperature. Mix and add powdered sugar and vanilla. Mix well and add remaining ingredients.

Chapter 21

What's Under the Frosting?

✳ ✳ ✳ ✳ ✳ ✳ ✳ ✳ ✳ ✳ ✳ ✳ ✳ ✳ ✳

During a driving trip through France, Harriet and I established a tradition, which we followed every morning. We would find the closest bakery or pastry shop and purchase fresh bread for our lunch and pastries to have with our morning coffee or hot chocolate. Purchasing a loaf of bread was usually easy, but selecting our pastries was a bit of a challenge. Because we speak absolutely no French beyond *merci* and *s'il vous plaît,* we took our chances by picking and pointing. We learned early on not to trust outside appearances. All too often, the beautifully sculpted chocolate icing covered a plain, overly sweet piece of pound cake. Some of the gorgeous combinations of fruit and whipped cream were no better. The outstanding choice of the entire trip was a rather plain-looking Danish with an almond stuffing that had us drooling every time we thought about it.

It might have helped, had we spoken the language, to know the ingredients in some of the pastries we chose; but in the end, how they tasted was all that really mattered. You can't judge a pastry by its frosting, but one bite tells you everything you need to know.

I suspect that if I were to ask my single and divorced patients how to choose a future spouse, most of them would say the same thing: "It's kind of like picking out a pastry in a French bakery when you don't speak the language."

Well, they might not say it exactly like that, but for the most part they would agree that it is a pick-and-point potluck process. And while initial attraction, chemistry, and good looks are certainly important, they would no doubt make it clear that—next time—they wouldn't make their decision based solely on outward appearance.

The ability to speak the same language helps considerably when purchasing pastries, but it is even more important in a marriage. Communication skills are a necessary quality to look for in a potential spouse. However, even there, what you see is not always what you get. I have frequently heard patients say about someone they are dating, "We can talk at length about anything. We stay on the phone for hours sharing our thoughts, our dreams, and our hopes for the future. What a difference from my ex-husband. We could drive for hours in the car and he'd never say a word unless I dragged it out of him."

My first thought is, *Sounds great, but will it last beyond the wedding ceremony?* Most lovers communicate pretty well with one another. It is husbands and wives who don't. Walk into any restaurant and look at the patrons. We can be certain that the ones who are gazing into each other's eyes and actively talking are single. The other couples, the ones who are more involved with the plate in front of them than with each other, are married. The question for the singles is, "How much of what is being said is truth and how much is fiction?"

I should point out that my earlier statement "You can't judge a pastry by its frosting, but one bite tells you every- thing you need to know" is a fallacy when applied to rela- tionships. I can't tell you how many singles I have known who justified sexual promiscuity, precocious sexual involvement, and moving in with one another, on the basis of "taking one bite" or having to "try it before you buy it." Studies have shown that the divorce rate for couples who live together before their marriage is far greater than the divorce rate for individuals who don't.

To my way of thinking, living with someone prior to marriage is only practice for living together; it isn't practice for being married to one another. If you want to know whether a successful marriage is possible with your lover, you have to run toward marriage. You can't just sniff at it, smell around the edges, and guess what it might be like. Most of us are too old to still be playing house. We should have done that as children. It's about time we invested ourselves in having the relationships we want, which means buying the pastry and taking a big bite out of it. ("Hey, this is mighty tasty!") Then we must expend the energy necessary to chew it thoroughly so that it's easy to swallow and digest, thereby releasing all the nourishment and contributing to our growth.

The process of picking a spouse is a scary one. As a result, many individuals have checklists they use to ensure that their choice of "Mr. or Ms. Right" is made on the basis of rational thinking rather than emotion. The lists that I have been privileged to see included such factors as educational level, type of profession or job, degree of ambition, dating history, early home life, emotional sensitivity, character, willingness to commit, attitude toward children, religious preference, ability to communicate, willingness to share feelings, and a host of other lesser criteria. All of these items are extremely important, but the list is of little significance when we try to determine how someone will interact with us in a marital relationship. Can we trust the honesty of our own answers to these questions, let alone trust our partner?

Let me illustrate my point with the words of one of my female patients. "All men are jerks. They lie, cheat, and steal. You can't believe them, trust them or let them out of your sight." From her statement, you might surmise that she is so bitter toward men that she wouldn't be interested in dating or marriage. Instead, she was totally conflicted. She would insist that men weren't worth having, but she was depressed because she didn't have one. But despite her desire for a relationship, she could hardly be seen as a positive partner

She went on to say that "All these jerks want is to get in your pants. Any one of my girlfriends will tell you the same thing. But I want more than that. The only problem is that I don't know how to tell what is really under the frosting—a gourmet chocolate torte or a fruitcake."

My response to her was the same as it would be today. "You think all men are jerks? So be it. We do have our flaws, our shortcomings and our unbridled sexual desires. I am sure that all your girlfriends would agree, but I am even more sorry that you choose women with those kind of attitudes to be your friends. Unfortunately, birds of a feather flock together to support each other's biased opinions, their fears of closeness, and their resentment toward men stemming from old hurts and experiences. I wonder if you wouldn't be better off emotionally with a new group of friends—women who would support you and help you to develop a more positive approach toward men in general and some man in particular."

Many men are jerks—I won't argue about that—but if women choose to live alone out of fear of being disappointed or hurt, they've chosen a poor solution to the situation. I believe I have a better one. If they're all jerks, go out and look for the best jerk you can find, one who is willing to learn, to grow, and to share the closeness you claim you want. If his first interest appears to be sex, be glad he finds you attractive and feels some chemistry with you. At the same time, recognize that you don't have to go to bed with him according to his timetable. Learn to say no, forcefully but with kindness. Then, if you can say it truthfully, let him know that you share his positive feelings. Tell him that although you have the same desires, your timetable doesn't coincide with his. Let him know that you are interested in developing every aspect of a close and loving relationship, and if he is willing to invest the time and energy necessary to build on a proper foundation, the two of you can work out the details together.

My patient also needed to know that men don't want a "pitiful pearl." Weak, dependent women are only a responsibility. They build a man up with statements like, "I am nothing without you," then weigh him down with the implied obligation that he must forever try to make them "something."

Most men cannot handle a partner who tells them, "You are the most wonderful person in the world. I am so lucky to have someone as great as you." These statements only serve to obligate a man to live up to the exaggerations. As a result, he feels he can never show his real self, lest the woman no longer adore him or look up to him.

Then, of course, there are those women who indicate initially how wonderfully capable a man is. They tell him that they admire him for all his potential, then after the rice is thrown, they begin to inform him, directly or indirectly, that he doesn't make enough money, he works too hard, and he isn't home enough. "And your children hardly know you." Only very sick jerks want that kind of woman.

What a well adjusted man wants is a partner who is already somebody. He wants a woman who can say, "I didn't marry Hemingway, Freud, or Dupont. I married you. I know your faults and your failings, but I also know your inner goodness and that is enough for me. I want to spend the rest of my life with you."

When a woman can honestly communicate her desires to her partner and honestly say that she wants him for who he is, she no longer has to worry about what is under the frosting. The fruitcakes will be scared away by her honesty. If a woman can be emotionally vulnerable, honest in communicating who she is, and capable of committing to an intimate relationship, she will attract men who are capable of these things as well. And let me say emphatically that everything I have suggested applies equally to men who are seeking an honest, well-adjusted woman When you discover that you are a "somebody" who can speak from the heart but knows how to use his head, you will spot the fruitcakes from a mile away— especially if she is dating a friend of yours. The only time we have a problem evaluating what is under the frosting is when we lose the struggle between our heads and our hearts. When we use our heads, decisions come easy. When our hearts come into play, facts can be distorted and issues confused because of biased views, emotional naïveté and childish attitudes.

The solution to the problem is obvious, but not easy. We have to discover that we are valuable and act on the basis of that newly discovered worth. Using your head in your relationships means to trust that you are worthy of love and to be honest with yourself and others.

Live well, eat well, and play well with the partner of your choice and cheat Father Time together. Most of all, steal each other's hearts. Keep them safe from harm. Soothe them when they hurt and celebrate with them when they rejoice.

Chocolate Mousse Pie

Crust
3 cups chocolate wafer crumbs
1/2 cup (1 stick) unsalted butter, melted
Filling
1 pound semisweet chocolate
2 eggs
4 egg yolks
2 cups whipping cream
6 tablespoons powdered sugar
4 egg whites, room temperature
Topping
2 cups whipping cream
sugar

Crust: Combine crumbs and butter. Press on bottom and completely up sides of a 10 inch springform pan. Refrigerate 30 minutes (or chill in freezer).

Filling: Soften chocolate in top of double boiler over simmering water. Let cool to lukewarm (95°). Add whole eggs and mix well. Add yolks and mix until thoroughly blended.

Whip cream with powdered sugar until soft peaks form. Beat eggs until stiff but not dry. Stir a little of cream and whites into chocolate mixture to lighten. Fold in remaining cream and whites until completely incorporated. Turn into crust and chill at least 6 hours, or overnight.

Topping: Whip remaining 2 cups cream with sugar to taste to stiff peaks.

Loosen crust on all sides using sharp knife; remove springform. Spread all the cream over the top.

Cut in wedges with a sharp knife. Serves 10–12.

Chapter 22

A Tall White Hat and an Apron Don't Make You a Chef

✳ ✳ ✳ ✳ ✳ ✳ ✳ ✳ ✳ ✳ ✳ ✳ ✳ ✳ ✳

One of my dearest friends, a Houston restaurateur, was asked to address a group of individuals who were about to become naturalized United States citizens. Each one had been in the United States for the prescribed length of time, had completed the necessary paperwork and had passed the mandatory exam. All that remained was for the presiding federal judge to swear them in. In his speech, my friend told them that from the moment they were sworn in they would be considered United States citizens, subject to the laws and benefits every citizen of this land enjoys. Along with the benefits, he added, come certain responsibilities of citizenship, such as voting, obeying the law, and upholding the Constitution. He assured them that when they left the courtroom, each of them could legally be called a United States citizen, but how deserving they were of that title could only be determined in the future. It would depend on the manner in which they lived up to their new responsibilities.

His words had a tremendous impact on me. I could see how they applied to every walk of life. We could graduate from cooking school, graduate school, or medical school, but the degree itself would not make us a chef, a teacher, a psychologist, an attorney, or a doctor. The way we practiced, the integrity we demonstrated, and the humanity we shared would determine whether we were genuinely worthy of our calling.

Of course, titles do not apply only to the workplace. Think of some of the other names we acquire in the course of a lifetime, such as daughter, son, father, mother, husband and wife. Biologically reproducing automatically makes us a mother or a father, but it takes far more effort, commitment and emotional investment to earn the title of parent.

It's the same for many of the other roles we fill in life. Saying "I do" makes you Mr. and Mrs., but learning how to be husband and wife is far more difficult. The groundwork was laid many years earlier when we observed our parents and we copied their behaviors by playing "house." When we became teenagers, we practiced close relationships through dating. Then we took the plunge for ourselves into marriage. In order to understand why we developed our particular style of loving and relating, we must recognize how our parents, friends, teachers, and society provided countless do's and don'ts that govern our sense of appropriate behavior. Ask anybody, regardless of age, social level or education, how to treat a spouse and the responses will be approximately the same. No one would condone yelling, screaming, hitting, abusing or ignoring your spouse. Everyone would agree that the way to go is to be considerate, kind, patient, caring, generous and loving.

We all know right from wrong. It's the doing of what we know that causes the problems we experience in life. Why? Because more often than not, our actions are not based on what we know. Instead, our actions are determined by how we feel, the inputs we retained from childhood, the situations in which we find ourselves, and the influence of those around us. In addition, the more stress we experience and the greater the anxiety we feel, the less we operate on the basis of our intelligence and the more our behavior is controlled by our emotions and patterned after the roles we learned both consciously and unconsciously during childhood.

We often see this truth demonstrated in professional sports. Athletes frequently taunt other players in an attempt to provoke their them. They know that if someone loses his temper or lets his emotions take over, he no longer plays smart. Both the game plan and long-term goals go out the window and the player acts in the heat of the moment on the basis of childhood inputs and immature motivations. Invariably, this form of behavior brings about self-defeating results.

I once saw a bright, articulate six-year-old young lady in therapy, whose stepmother had just moved her father out of their home. She then replaced him with a man ten years her junior. In relating the story to me, the girl said, "My real mom told me that the new man doesn't even have a car or a job."

"What do you think about that" I asked.

"I'll never move in with someone who doesn't have a car or a job," she replied.

Enough said. At age six, she had already stored away a block of information. It's all right to move someone out; it's all right to move someone in; but he must have a car and a job. Without her even being aware, her memory bank received a deposit regarding how to act in a relationship. It would not surprise me to hear someday, maybe ten or fifteen years down the road, that she has acted based on that input.

"Strong on form but weak on substance" aptly described Chuck and Karen. Both were attractive and personable college graduates who had achieved success in their careers. At one time, they genuinely thought they were in love with each other. They dreamed of building a lifetime together and expected to be married forever. Twelve years, two children, four moves, and one affair later, they decided to try therapy.

For Karen, the transition from full-time career woman to full time homemaker was very difficult. She walked away from a lucrative and challenging job, surrendering up her financial independence, and now had to rely on Chuck to support the family. Trusting dependence ran contrary to everything she had learned as a child.

The changes were just as difficult for Chuck. Suddenly, he found himself the sole support of the family. Despite outward appearances to the contrary, he was constantly fearful that, like his father, he would prove an inadequate provider. To Chuck, nothing could be worse. He had grown up with a mother who constantly complained about everything they didn't have. "Every chance she had" he said," she reminded me and the rest of the kids how much of a disappointment Dad was. No matter what we asked for, she only had one answer. If Daddy made more money we could get that for you."

Now, in his own marriage, Chuck became extraordinarily sensitive every time Karen mentioned expenses, bills or credit cards. To combat his anxiety, he decided to take over control of all the finances, even though Karen was far better at organizing and dealing with details. When things became tough or he felt a financial squeeze, he let off steam by becoming obsessed with her spending. He often launched into tirades about how she wasn't sticking to the budget; he ranted and raved about the cost of the furniture she bought for the living room; and he criticized her decision to continue to drive the luxury car she had purchased when she was still working outside the home.

At the same time, he responded to his fear of being perceived as an inadequate provider by, paradoxically, making major expenditures of his own that they could ill afford. He bought a new car, even though the monthly payments were more than they could comfortably handle, and a powerboat that constantly needed repairs. Even though their house was far larger than they needed—and had a hefty mortgage to go with it—the stigma of "trading down" ruled out any kind of move.

Over the years, the pressure increased. Always a social drinker, Chuck began staying out late with the guys and frequently came home less than sober. He complained, to anyone who would listen, Karen was never satisfied no matter how much he gave her. Through seemingly humorous remarks, he frequently portrayed her as a gold digger who thought she was married to Rockefeller. The more inadequate he felt, the more insufficient he made his wife out to be.

Chuck's behavior pattern is not uncommon and serves several purposes. It can be an unconscious attempt to alienate a spouse to the point that he or she will be the one to leave, thereby becoming the instigator of disunion. It can also be seen as a defensive behavior, akin to saying, "You can't fire me, I quit." Or it can simply be a case of building yourself up by tearing someone else down

In any case, the behavior stems from an intense feeling of inadequacy, not a lack of love. But no matter what the source is, the outcome is usually the demise of the relationship. In Chuck's case, he met a secretary at the company, who was sympathetic, consoling, and a willing, enthusiastic sex partner.

Eventually, the secretary wrote a letter to Karen saying,"How could a woman living in a four-hundred-thousand dollar house, driving a Lexus and playing tennis three times a week at the country club complain about anything? If I were married to Chuck, I would certainly appreciate him for everything he provides." What she didn't realize, was that if she were married to Chuck, she would probably become the butt of his remarks. She would have been the person who had to live with his emotional mood swings, and his ranting and raving. And she would have become the woman who felt rejected because of his long periods of silence, his lack of communication, and his sullen attitude.

The letter was the last straw. It gave Karen all the resolve she needed to make her decision. She was finally going to get out. It wasn't the first time she had thought about it. In fact, it had crossed her mind many times since early in the marriage. She thought, "Men find me attractive, I'm personable and a lot of fun. I can easily return to the work force, and with child support and a salary, I can make it. I'll have no financial problems. As far as the kids go, I'm the one who has raised them and tended to their problems. I can still be there for them."

As long as she was angry, she remained confident and undaunted by her decision to file for a divorce. As the days went by, however, she began to remember the good times. She thought about how difficult it would be for her children to live in a single parent home. She started to fear going out into the single world. She asked herself, "How can I avoid making the same mistake again? I never thought Chuck would do what he did. How could I ever trust another man?

Maybe I'm better off staying with the devil I know than finding a devil I don't know." All these thoughts and a thousand more began swirling around in her head. She tried her best to stay angry so she could stay focused, but increasingly the anger was replaced by fear and sadness.

To make matters worse, a vaguely familiar feeling in the pit of her stomach reminded her of how she felt while she was growing up. She had always blamed her emotional problems on her father for leaving, but when she examined her feelings in therapy, she discovered a layer of resentment against her mother for all the other men she had allowed into their home. Most of these men had treated her more harshly and critically than her father ever had, yet her mother rarely intervened or stood up to protect her. She recalled feeling totally alone and clearly remembered the day she had consciously decided that she would never fully trust anyone again.

Throughout their marriage, Chuck very likely sensed, at some level of consciousness, that she was not totally committed. At the same time, his behavior confirmed Karen's belief and fear that she could not emotionally depend on anyone. Chuck certainly wasn't there for her; nevertheless, his critical comments, rejection of her and lack of communication wasn't unbearable. Reminiscent of her childhood, it was painful, but familiar. It was the devil she knew and the devil she anticipated.

When they came in for therapy, they each brought enough baggage that it wasn't a case of who was right and who was wrong. They blamed each other, but I'm convinced that no matter who else they would have married, they would have experienced similar problems. They each needed to grapple with substantial issues within themselves before they could constructively work together on their marriage. How they will do remains to be seen.

Emotionally speaking, few of us ever go beyond our childhood beliefs and fears. These ingrained responses hamper our ability to behave in accordance with what we know and who we are. We hide behind invisible shields, seeking the approval of others and portraying ourselves as images of who we wish were. Chuck unconsciously expects every female he loves to act like his mother—dissatisfied, disgruntled, and always finding fault. In response—or in anticipation—he assumes the role of an agreeable, non-communicating husband, who hides his anger and resentment and buries his inner thoughts and opinions. Karen is convinced that if you begin to trust or lean on someone, you can be sure that he will find fault with you and disappoint you over time. Her shield is to appear to be the perfect woman, wife and mother on the surface. While she plays the role, however, she rigorously protects her emotions.

The perceptions that are driving Chuck and Karen's behavior are as erroneous as the assumption that every person in a white chef's hat can make a perfect soufflé. The problem is, it's far easier to become *something* than it is to be *someone*. When our identity is tied up in what we do, we can never afford for our image to be blemished. Any chink in our armor is seen as a flaw in ourselves. Consequently, most of our energies and efforts end up directed toward building, enhancing or protecting our image rather than interacting with others or giving of ourselves to someone else.

Without an integrated sense of self and self esteem, everything we go into, whether it be a career, a relationship or a marriage, becomes something we have to draw from or live through, not something we can invest in, build on, or share with others. To develop a sense of self requires that we see the person behind the chef who makes the souffle. The souffle does not make the chef. In a marriage, our inherent sense of worth or value is what allows us to make our marriage exciting and rewarding—which is the result of investing ourselves—rather than looking to our marriage or our spouse to make us feel that we are of value. If we are struggling in our marriage, we often must first "go in" before we can come out.

"Going in" is another way of saying we must discover ourselves. The steps required are similar to those involved in making a pie. The first thing we have to do is make a sturdy, flavorful crust to hold the filling. To make a simple crust, we need water, butter, flour and a little salt. We've all been told at one time or another that we're "all wet," so coming up with the water is no problem. Butter is the element in the crust that holds the other ingredients together. Butter is simply cream that has been shaken up or agitated. If we can turn the turmoil of our past experiences into something useful and create something tasty, we will have gained a measure of redemption in our lives. Flour is the basic meal, the goodness in every one of us. Add a little salt for spice and we have the makings of a good crust.

The next step requires muscle, the hard work involved in kneading the ingredients together and rolling out the dough into the shape we want us to be. The final step is to pour in our hopes, dreams and wishes, and then apply sufficient energy—hot or cold—to solidify the contents into a delicious confection worthy of a strong cup of coffee.

How does this work in real life? A ballet dancer whose sole support in life is her dancing develops arthritis and can no longer dance. Does she fall apart? Does she crumble into a terrible mess? If she has a solid sense of herself and a savory feeling of worth as a person, perhaps she utilizes her talent and her years of experience to become a choreographer.

The point is, she is not an empty shell. She has a solid foundation that keeps her together and provides her with a foundation on which to build something new. Even if we don't have a good pre-baked shell from our youth, it is never too late to scuttle around in the pantry and make one. We first have to look inside to recognize that, despite our shortcomings and our fears, we all have some cream and some basic starch in us. The water may come from our tears, but when everything is kneaded together with a zest for life, we end up with a crust ready for filling. And if anyone suggests that we're flaky—well, that's a compliment for pie shells like us. Don't get discouraged, just smile and keep moving along.

Once the crust is prepared, all that remains is to add the delicious filling that will make us a mouth-watering treat for our loved ones to enjoy. Live well, love others, and you'll get your just desserts.

Shelly's Easy Finger Licking Good Coffee Cake

Every once in a while we come across a person who is just what he or she appears to be. He looks like, acts like and really is a chef. Well this recipe is just what it says. I got it from my daughter Shelly. It is finger licking good, and it is so easy you don't expect it to be half as good as it is. When you bring it to the table, no one will believe that you made it. It is a winner in every way. The very next time you give a large family breakfast or brunch, trust me enough to try it. I promise you will be as pleased as your guests.

1 package frozen TV dinner rolls (your favorite brand)
1 cup sugar & 1 heaping tablespoon cinnamon mixed
1 cup chopped pecans
1 cup raisins
1 package butterscotch pudding mix (not instant)
2 cups brown sugar
1-1/4 sticks butter

Grease a bundt pan and place frozen dinner rolls on bottom. Pour the sugar and cinnamon mixture on the dinner rolls. Sprinkle the chopped pecans and raisins over the top. Now sprinkle the butterscotch pudding mix, next add the brown sugar on top of the pudding mix. Slice the butter and place evenly on top. Place it in a cold oven overnight to rise. The next morning, remove pan while you preheat oven to 350° then bake it for 30 minutes. Remove from oven and turn it over on a plate. Looks and tastes great!

Chapter 23

More Can Be Too Much

✳   ✳   ✳   ✳   ✳   ✳   ✳   ✳   ✳   ✳   ✳   ✳   ✳   ✳   ✳

Palm Springs is a wonderful place to visit. Lemons, grapefruit, oranges, and tangerines all seem to grow without effort. Baskets of citrus were scattered throughout the home of our friends who had invited us for an extended weekend. Twice a day, they squeezed lemons as big as our fists and made pitchers of the most delicious lemonade I have ever tasted. Maybe it was the atmosphere or the company, but I swear their lemons grow sweeter than anywhere else I have been.

The second day, our host added a small amount of chopped fresh grapefruit meat to the lemonade. Amid lip-smacking accolades, the oversized pitcher emptied in record time. That very evening he repeated the process with adding slightly more grapefruit, while everyone at the table sang his praises with even greater gusto.

On the third day, however, the lemonade pitcher was left standing more than three-quarters full on the breakfast table. Our enthusiastic lemonade sommelier had gone too far. The wonderful lemon juice had been all but replaced by bitter grapefruit pulp. More of a good thing had indeed become too much.

The lemonade incident presents a microscopic picture of typical human behavior. Perhaps you've complimented a woman for her delicate and subtle perfume, only to have her breeze in the next morning in an eye-watering cloud of fragrance. Or maybe you know a man who was praised for his sense of humor as a youngster, and who now plays the role of office clown and substitutes conversation with jokes. Or a young woman whose parents reinforced her budding sexuality with comments such as, "By the time you're twenty, you will leave a trail of broken hearts behind you." Today, she dresses provocatively and reinforces her ego through sexual innuendo. All three are victims of the idea that if a little bit is good, more is better.

In cooking, too much salt, hot pepper sauce, or oregano can easily spoil a dish. In life, too much anger, saccharine sweetness, or possessiveness can ruin a relationship. We all know people who fit this pattern. One drink is never enough. It always leads to being drunk. One spoonful of ice cream is only a taste. It takes a pint to satisfy their appetite. One quip that elicits attention from a dinner crowd is repeated ad nauseam. Children frequently overact. They say or do something once and if you smile, laugh, or compliment them, they repeat the statement or action to the point that it becomes obnoxious and negative.

A young patient of mine brought his girlfriend with him to a therapy session. He had the air of an injured puppy and spoke with a whiny voice. She was his first love and he was totally dismayed. How could she possibly say that he loved her too much? He could not fathom why calling his girlfriend two or three times a day would bother her. If she really loved him, why wouldn't she want to talk to him as often as he wanted to talk to her? Even more hurtful was how she sometimes shrugged him off when he hugged her, complaining that he was either smothering her or hanging on her.

She insisted that she loved him and that she was resisting his dependent behavior not rejecting his love, but he could not comprehend what she was saying. Perhaps it was too difficult for him to admit to his dependency. Nevertheless, it was painfully apparent that any more of his love would eventually drive her away.

In all these situations, more was definitely not better. But excessive behavior can be used to make a diagnosis. It can signify how needy, dependent or depressed a person really is. For people who don't know when to stop, more is not only not better, it is sadly never enough.

Steve and June were two examples of this phenomenon. June was the daughter of middle class parents who ran their own successful business. She was the classic middle child, who felt overlooked, lost in the shuffle and lacking in self-worth, despite her intelligence and attractiveness. As a child, she tried everything to gain attention and to take center stage, but to no avail. Her older brother— the first born son—could do no wrong in his parent's eyes. June's younger sister was the baby of the family and everybody's darling. June, at least to her way of thinking, was lost somewhere in the middle. To compensate, she became a sophisticated clown, a master of sharp wit and a femme fatale. She excelled at each role but she never knew when to quit. Her humor was at times critical and hurtful, and her seductive attire was often embarrassing and inappropriate. Her behavior attracted the attention she desperately desired, but her inner sadness, her painful neediness, and her feelings of inadequacy were left clearly exposed.

She paid a terrible price for a moment in the highly fickle limelight. She held center stage, but the attention she received was primarily negative and deprecatory. What she didn't realize was that inside her was a wonderful, kind, sensitive human being, who was valuable in her own right; a person who could be loved and appreciated for who and what she really was, if only she were willing to give her real self a chance.

Steve's behavior was at the opposite end of the spectrum. He too was a middle child who saw most of the attention in his family directed toward his older brother and younger sister. That attention, however, was not positive. His mother was an unhappy, disgruntled woman, whose perceptions were filtered through dark glasses. She was frightened of the world and compensated for her fear by attempting to control the people and the environment around her. She cut her husband and children very little slack. She could be rigidly domineering and occasionally abusive, frequently contemptuous of their thoughts, opinions, and behaviors. On the surface, she might have been viewed as a caring, concerned, and loving mother, who gathered her chicks around her in a tight circle in order to protect them from others, even their father. To my way of thinking, however, she was an iron fist in a terry cloth glove.

Steve always spoke highly of his mother and thought of her as an angel; but when she died, he began to see for the first time how her presence and her attitudes had colored his life. Steve had always thought of his father as cold and distant. Now that he was able to interact with his father one on one, Steve discovered he was surprisingly warm and responsive. As we discussed his upbringing, Steve began to see, albeit reluctantly, how his mother's influence had played a role in his brother's divorce and how it influenced his own problems with his wife.

The purpose behind uncovering these links was not to discredit his mother or malign her. Instead, I was trying to help Steve to understand his own behavior in his marriage. With his wife, he was a non-opinionated, non-communicative, slow thinking, forgetful, insensitive, passive individual. He had learned early in life that being agreeable and not communicating enabled him to move through life without hurt or criticism. This strategy had served him well as a child. He had escaped his mother's wrath by developing an air of invisibility, which protected him from her bitter tirades. No wonder he brought the same behavior to his marriage. At work, he was a radically different man. On the job, he felt safe, competent and free from his emotional fears. Consequently, he was able to risk failure and to behave with confidence.

Steve's lack of involvement in his marriage allowed him to sidestep negative reactions from his wife. However, it also eliminated any positive feelings he might have experienced at home. He settled for behaving out of fear. He took no emotional risks and thus avoided emotional pain. Nevertheless, he paid a price. His agreeable passivity cast him in an acquiescent, compliant role,which filled him with resentment for his wife and contempt for himself. Unable or unwilling to express his feeling openly, he buried them.

Both June and Steve harbored deep feelings of anger that they were unable to consciously acknowledge to themselves. Steve's inner feelings of anger and depression came out through forgetfulness, lack of sensitivity and seemingly mindless statements. His passive-aggressive behavior contrasted 180 degrees from June's thinly veiled hostility, which she cloaked in sharp-tongued humor.

Both Steve and June felt poorly about themselves, but instead of looking for a new perspective or new ways to express themselves, they both tried the "more of the same" strategy. She became more flirtatious, more humorous, and more insidiously hostile. He became more silent, more introspective and more preoccupied. Like grapefruit pulp added to already tart lemonade, the result was bitter disappointment.

Fortunately, June married a man who needed her flamboyant facade. In a highly neurotic sense, he basked in the leftover limelight that reflected from her persona, but at the same time he resented that he could not fully satisfy her needs for attention. As a result, in the role he played out, he tended to either ignore her or to subtly criticize her with a dry wit that cut her while for the most part going over the heads of others. Without realizing, she replicated in her marriage the same relationship she had experienced with her mother, her father, and her siblings. To make matters even worse, in search of help, June went from one therapist to another looking for a sympathetic "friend" who would laugh at her humor, provide her with attention and take her side in conflict situations. Although this type of therapeutic relationship may be very comforting, it is seldom conducive to growth or change.

Meanwhile, Steve continued his ineffectual existence until his wife finally filed for divorce. It took that cold splash of reality for Steve to open his eyes to himself and his behavior. Now that he was awake, he began to own up to his feelings of weakness and his fear of confrontation with anyone he loved. He acknowledged his dread of possible rejection and his self-hatred because of his inability to stand up for himself. To his utter surprise, his wife did not reject his halting efforts to change. Instead, she

loved and accepted him for his openness and honesty.
Today, their marriage is better than it has ever been. The
process was slow but positive. It involved taking three steps
forward and an occasional two steps back. Steve learned
that more defensiveness, more denial and more sulking was
far too much. I hope that June will come to the same realization herself someday.

In the kitchen, the ingredients we add to the basic
dish should only be those that complement or enhance the
flavor of the food. In life, we often add the wrong ingredient in the wrong amount, kind of like pouring in a cup of
salt when the recipe calls for a tablespoon of sugar. When
we lack confidence in ourselves we exaggerate our actions,
our accomplishments, our strengths and our importance.
When we feel low, we attack others by embarrassing them,
deprecating them, or otherwise declaring our superiority
over them. In these examples, our behavior only serves to
bring embarrassment to us and to more clearly highlight
the very feelings of insufficiency and insecurity we are
attempting to hide.

A dear friend of mine has a saying that well describes
this behavior. He says, "You can talk so much that you go
from right to wrong with your mouth." Unfortunately, when
we do not appreciate who we are, we fall back on our old
behaviors. It is not easy to change these patterns, but change
is essential. You see, my friend's saying is true in reverse as
well. We can go from wrong to right by saying less, by
exposing our inner selves more, and by letting our actions
speak for us. Suddenly, we no longer need to try so hard or
so much.

Unfortunately, some people never reach that place.
Countless wives and husbands endure years of marriage
resenting how much they have given and how little they

have received in return. Their laments read like a typical romance novel. "I catered to his every whim. I cooked a hot dinner every night. I cared for the children's needs. I never refused him sex and what did I get in return? I'll tell you: nothing. He worked. He played golf. He traveled. He ate out in fancy restaurants. Meanwhile, I was the cook, the maid and the nanny. I tried harder and harder but I could never please him."

On the other side of the marital bed is a guy who feels exactly the same way. "I am nothing but a money machine. I work hard. I support my family, the maid, the beautician, the piano teacher, the gym coach, the dance teacher, and the orthodontist, not to mention the pediatrician, the gardener, and the stockholders of several grocery chains. Then there's Saks, Lord & Taylor, Penney's and Neiman Marcus. I'm called on to take care of every problem and I'm not allowed to go home, sit down with a drink and watch the evening news on TV. I am told that I never spend time with the kids, the car won't start, and I promised to barbecue tonight. There is no rest for the weary and no slack or consideration for my interests. I have to beg for a weekend fishing trip. I can't smoke because it isn't healthy and if I take two drinks, it's time for me to attend AA meetings. Nothing I do pleases her. No matter how much money I make, it's never enough, and I sometimes ask myself, 'What's it all for?'"

Both parties feel cheated and trapped. Both are resentful and emotionally vulnerable to the attraction of another person—you know, that special someone who would appreciate everything he or she did. Once again, more proves to be too much. The more we try to find our identity through our spouse's attention, the more we end up resenting his or her lack of appreciation, until it finally becomes too much. But even if we had received it, the attention would never have been sufficient or lasted long enough to be of real satisfaction. Think about it. No one can give to us what we need to discover within ourselves. If I try for years to do for you to get for me, am I really giving or taking? Also, if I resent you in proportion to what I have given, how much of myself have I withheld, consciously or not, to fuel my anger?

Only when we learn to truly value ourselves, with all our shortcomings, weaknesses and failings, can we give ourselves to others in proper measure. When we see that a little less is just right, we can cease striving and simply enjoy ourselves and our revitalized relationships.

Rice Pudding Crème Brûlée

This is the exception to the rule. More is never too much of this dessert. It is one of my favorites. Harriet frequently makes it for me when she serves one of her fabulous chocolate desserts to others. You see, I am one of the few individuals who is not a chocoholic.

2/3 cup water
1/3 cup long grain rice
2 cups milk
1/2 cup heavy cream
1 vanilla bean split lengthwise
2 large whole eggs
3 large egg yolks
1/4 teaspoon cinnamon
1/4 teaspoon nutmeg
1/2 cup raisins
1/2 cup honey
1/4 teaspoon salt
1/3 cup firmly packed light brown sugar

Bring water to a boil in a small pan, add rice and a pinch of salt. Simmer gently covered, for 15 to 20 minutes until water is absorbed. Place rice in a bowl and cool.

Preheat oven to 300°. Butter a 9-inch glass baking dish. In a pan bring the milk and the cream to a boil, add the vanilla bean and remove from heat. Scrape the seeds from the vanilla bean into the milk mixture, discard pod. In a bowl whisk together the whole eggs, egg yolks, nutmeg, raisins, honey, and salt. Add the rice and blend well, pour the milk in a stream whisking all the while. Pour custard into the baking dish which has been placed in a pan. Add sufficient hot water to the pan to reach halfway up the side of the custard dish. Bake in the middle of the oven for 60 to 70 minutes or until custard is set. Transfer the custard to a rack and cool. Cover and chill in refrigerator for at least 6 hours or overnight.

Just before serving, sprinkle the brown sugar through a coarse sieve on the top of the custard. To crisp, set the custard dish in a baking dish filled with ice and place below a hot broiler for 2 to 3 minutes. Should you decide to prepare this dish again—and I promise you will once you taste it—invest in a small blow torch. Chefs use a torch for melting and crisping brown sugar toppings, as well as for browning meringues. It is easy to use, takes only a minute, requires no fussing with baking plans and ice and almost entirely eliminates the problem of burning a meringue or topping. This recipe serves 8 to 10 but can easily be doubled.

Chapter 24

The Very Best Gift

❊ ❊ ❊ ❊ ❊ ❊ ❊ ❊ ❊ ❊ ❊ ❊ ❊ ❊

It was the last married couples meeting before Christmas. The group members were seated on a circular couch surrounding an oversized lazy Susan. I was sitting in an upholstered swivel chair, facing the group with my back to the door. I heard the door being eased open. I turned to see a hand slowly snake through the narrow opening holding a large sugar cone with two dips of rum raisin ice cream. Without hesitation, I reached out and grasped the cone. The hand gently released its hold, the arm withdrew and the door closed. The incident was over almost as quickly as it had begun but the feelings are still with me today. I can still recall licking the dribbles of melted ice cream that slowly made their way down the sides of the cone. As I savored each creamy bite, the emotional realization of what had taken place hit me. I hadn't been handed a rum raisin ice cream cone. I had received a double dip of love.

We were discussing that evening the difficulty of buying gifts during the holiday season. Several individuals mentioned how much easier it had become since they had overcome their fear of buying the wrong size, the wrong color, or something the recipient might not like. Others nodded in agreement and added that their own fears stemmed from feelings of inadequacy. They felt that their gifts had to be perfect to make up for their feelings of insufficiency. One person said, "The more fear I feel before buying a gift, the more I tend to spend.It's almost as though I'm saying, 'Well if they don't like it at least they'll appreciate how much I spent.'"

With her simple act of love, expressed in that ice cream cone, my wife, Harriet had provided us with a shining example of gift-giving based on her strength. She knew that Baskin Robbins and Haägen Dazs make rum raisin ice cream every Christmas season. I eagerly await this yearly luxury and indulge myself with delight. No words were needed, no prolonged glances exchanged or verbalized appreciation expressed. Her gift spoke volumes and reached deep into my soul. It was a gift I have never forgotten. It said, "I know you. I love you. You're worth the thought, the time, and the effort."

Her gift contained the essence of everything I try to teach my patients in therapy: When you care for someone, show it openly, courageously and emotionally. Don't question or worry about the other person's actions or behaviors. Harriet's gift portrayed all of the positive dynamics involved in giving your loved ones the three best presents they will ever receive —none of which is a double dip of rum raisin ice cream.

The first gift is *encouraging your loved ones to have the freedom to be themselves.* This is not an easy gift to give. You must first be prepared to give up control. You must be emotionally secure enough to live with someone who behaves in an independent manner; someone whose words, actions and thoughts may be at odds with your own. The gift of freedom is difficult for individuals with any feelings of insecurity—which includes most of us.

Early in my marriage, I had the peculiar notion that if my wife truly loved me, she would share my opinions, like the same kind of food I did and enjoy the same kind of people. Anyone who knows my wife and me also knows the sheer lunacy of my expectations. They also know that her sense of individuality does not diminish the love she has for me. I sometimes forget. I resort to the cliché that "If she loved me, she would also love my dog."

Today, I recognize that when I have that thought, I have emotionally regressed and my feelings of insecurity have taken over. It is ironic, but nevertheless true, that when a person feels emotionally sufficient and worthy of being loved, it is easy to "permit" others to have their own opinions, thoughts, and positions. It is only when we feel insecure and unloved that the statement "If you loved me, you would agree with me" seems true instead of the emotional illusion it is.

It is important to add that, within the context of this illusion, control by any other name is still control. No matter how we cloak our good intentions, saying such things as "I want to help you learn from my past experience" or "I'm simply trying to protect you from the pain or failures I experienced," control is control. Because of that, as givers of this gift we must realize that even the freedom to err, to make mistakes and learn from them, is far more valuable than the benefit derived from "well-intended attempts" to help others avoid the pitfalls in life. Too often, our "help" results in the recipient having to give up their freedom, remain a child, and accept being controlled. In the end, they wind up resenting the providers of these "well-intended suggestions."

Another factor to be considered is that some recipients of the gift of freedom are not overly anxious to have it. Unconsciously, they may prefer their dependency. They may be willing to be dependent rather than have to take responsibility for themselves. Meanwhile, they shout to the world their resentment of control and their desire for freedom. If the truth were known, most of these self-perceived victims are too frightened to live independently. Thus, in order to give someone his freedom, you must be emotionally strong enough yourself to give up control, and the heir to your gift must be capable of receiving it. The act of letting go becomes a testimony to the giver's own growth and a catalyst that enables the benefactor to grow as well.

The second gift is *giving of yourself.* Initially, this gift sounds relatively simple, but in order to give yourself away, you must first have possession of yourself. You can't give away something that you don't own. To own yourself requires that you know yourself and have insight into yourself. Most of us are too frightened to look at or to accept our own feelings of fear, insufficiency or lack of worth. Consequently we are unable to share.

It follows, then, that before you can possibly give yourself to someone else, you must first give yourself to you. That's the hardest gift of all to give. Despite intellectual awareness to the contrary, we tend to expect perfection in ourselves, and anything that falls short is unacceptable. No wonder we feel unacceptable to someone else. For that reason, few people ever reveal all of themselves to those they love.

In couples therapy, it is not unusual to hear a distraught spouse say, "You don't understand me. All these years and you have no idea who and what I am." The statement is usually intended as a condemnation of the other person; but in reality, it is more often a condemnation of the one speaking. It says "I have never let you know who I am, because I have never felt I would be acceptable in your eyes." In the heartwarming Christmas story about the gift of the Littlest Angel, we learn that despite the meagerness of the gift, it was valued because the Littlest Angel gave what was dearest to himself. Perhaps, all of us can learn a lesson from this; that each of us must come to see and feel our own worth in spite of our inner fears and feelings of insufficiency. We must come to recognize that no one is perfect but each of us must find value in ourselves. Only when you come to realize and accept yourself for who you are will you become a valuable gift to someone else.

The third gift is the *gift of reality.* It is probably the most important gift you can give to your partner, your children, your friends, and yourself. I discussed this gift at some length in the chapter called "Cottage Cheese Therapy," but in the context of this chapter I want to add a few thoughts. The first step in giving the gift of reality is seeking to understand your spouse or other loved one. By learning the way to your loved one's heart—and then trying to get there—you establish the basis for loving confrontation inherent in giving the gift of reality.

When Harriet loaded the refrigerator with umpteen cartons of cottage cheese, she was speaking to me in terms that I could understand. She was saying, "I know that you love me more than cottage cheese, but if you're not quite so sure yourself, pop open a few cartons and see." When we take the time to understand our spouse, we develop and demonstrate the level of love, tenderness and commitment necessary to wrap the gift of reality.

During the next holiday season or your next special day, don't let stress cause you to miss the spirit of the occasion. Take time to consider the three most valuable gifts you can give to another: the gift of freedom, the gift of yourself, and the gift of reality. Remember that giving these gifts requires that you be honestly introspective, have the courage of your convictions and the fortitude to risk rejection. Try to let go of control, give a double dip of a delectable "you" to someone else and show tender honesty with everyone. Wrap these gifts with vulnerability, care and love. Scoop into a large sugar cone and eventually the gift cannot help but reap reciprocal loving emotions.

Rum Raisin Ice Cream

3/4 cup raisins
1/4 cup rum
2 tablespoons brewed English Breakfast tea
4 large egg yolks
3/4 cup sugar
1-1/4 cups milk
1 tablespoon unsalted butter
1 two-inch piece of vanilla bean
1-1/4 cups chilled heavy cream

Chop raisins. In a small bowl, soak raisins in rum and tea for 2 hours. In another bowl, with an electric mixer, beat yolks with sugar until thick and pale yellow. In a 2 to 3 quart heavy saucepan bring milk and butter with vanilla bean just to a boil. Add hot milk mixture to yolks in a slow stream while whisking, and transfer to pan. Cook over moderately low heat stirring constantly, until it reaches a temperature of 170°F. Stir in raisin mixture and cook custard completely. Chill mixture (cover surface with plastic wrap) until cold, about 1 hour.

In a bowl, with cold beaters, mix cream until it begins to thicken. Stir into custard and combine well. Freeze in an ice-cream maker. Transfer ice cream to an airtight container and put in freezer. Makes about 1 quart.

Chapter 25

Soul Food

✳ ✳ ✳ ✳ ✳ ✳ ✳ ✳ ✳ ✳ ✳ ✳ ✳ ✳ ✳

Soul food conjures up images of fried chicken, mashed potatoes, greens and corn bread, which for some people is the purest form of Southern style home cooking. For others, soul food is matzo ball soup and flanken, chile rellenos and beans, corned beef and cabbage, or pasta with a heavy tomato-meat sugo. Whatever the culture and whatever the food, the most important element is the expression of love that fills our stomachs and warms our hearts.

In leaner times there wasn't much to work with, but our mothers knew how to stretch things and how to make leftovers taste even better than the original. The secret is working with what we have and serving everything with a large scoop of love. If your life is filled with hurried schedules, fast food, and recycled relationships—and who among us doesn't suffer from at least one or two of these?— you need to slow down and at least once a week take the time to mix up enough "Loving Cordial" to last for the next seven days.

A Loving Cordial

1 large portion of demonstrative emotion (be generous)
1 equal portion of sugar (do not use a sugar substitute)
1 large serving of attention and time (a small amount of
    "quality time" is not an adequate substitute, it is only
    a rationalization)
1 equal portion of honesty (not hostility)
1 generous serving of kindness, concern, and care

Strain emotions several times, being certain to remove any trace of old hurts, anger, fear, and resentment. Combine with the remaining four ingredients. Mix well. Place in a receptive heart and heat over a low burner to a warm temperature. Serve to everyone you care for and be prepared to give large portions and second helpings. I promise it will be returned to you tenfold.